INFORMATION TECHNOLOGY IN 21ST CENTURY

INFORMATION TECHNOLOGY IN 21ST CENTURY

(In 9 Volumes)

TECHNOLOGY TRENDS OF INFORMATION TECHNOLOGY

(Volume 5)

PROF. RAMESH CHANDRA

Vice-Chancellor, Bundelkhand University, Jhansi (U.P.)

Publication

KALPAZ PUBLICATIONS

DELHI-110052

INFORMATION TECHNOLOGY IN 21ST CENTURY
Technology Trends of Information Technology
(Information Technolgy)

Rs. 8000 (Set)
Rs. 900 (each volume)

ISBN: 81-7835-158-7 (Set)
ISBN: 81-7835-163-3 (Vol. 5)

Published in 2003 in India by
Kalpaz Publications
C-30, Satyawati Nagar
Delhi-110052
E-mail: kalpaz@hotmail.com

Laser Typesetting at: A.S. Printers
Printed at: Chawla Offset Printers, Delhi

Preface

In the last hundred years, we see the rapidly accelerating advent of a technology so powerful, novel, widespread, and influential that we may indeed call it the second industrial revolution. Its basis is electromagnetic, in many interconnected forms: photography, telegraphy, radio communication, radar, sound and video recording, transistors, printed circuits, integrated circuits (IC), very large-scale integration (VLSI) of circuitry on a tiny semi-conducting 'chip', the bewildering variety of electronic digital computers, and finally the internet.

The internet is a massive global network of interconnected packet-switched computer networks. There is no agreed-upon definition because the internet is at once a set of common protocols, a physical collection of routers and circuits, distributed resources, and even a culture of connectivity and communications. The most exciting commercial developments are occurring on that portion of the Internet known as the World Wide Web (WWW). The WWW is a distributed hypermedia environment within the Internet. Global hypermedia allows multimedia information to be located on a network of servers around the world which are interconnected, allowing one to travel through the information by clicking on hyperlinks. Any hyperlink can point to any document anywhere on the Internet. The present popularity of the WWW as a commercial medium is due to its ability to facilitate global sharing of information and resources, and its potential to provide an efficient channel for advertising, marketing, and even direct distribution of certain goods and information services.

The digital revolution combined with the setting up of open, interconnected, interactive networks has fostered a number of radical changes, the most important of which have resulted in the dematerialisation of products, growing concentration in cultural sectors and the globalisation of communication networks. The Internet has created an environment that makes that statement truer than at any prior point. The Internet enables incredibly fast access to an enormous amount of information and provides connectivity and community that can empower buyers.

This book offers the most thorough treatment available on the technology trends and its applications in the infoage. It will be useful and valuable for both students and researchers, as we well as professionals, information technologists and communicators.

Editor

Contents

1

Introduction

We are living in a cyber world, were scientific and technological advancements produced widespread impacts on society. The utility of computers doubled by the introduction of the global telecommunication network, which forms a platform for internet. Internet made it possible to easily pass large quantity of information at a comparatively 'less time less cost formula'. The concept of a decentralised computer network had been considered by a number of countries.

Usenet

Usenet is a facility accessed via the Internet. It is a world wide information exchange or news system allowing you to read, contribute and reply to letters or as on allmost every topic you can imagine. Usenet is sometimes called network news or net news. The postings are divided into newsgroups each devoted to a certain topic. There are several thousand news groups arranged hierarchically. Not all sites on the network receive all the news groups.

A site may choose which groups it wishes to receive. and individuals may choose which of those groups received by their site that they actually want to see. Several hundred megabytes of news is posted to Usenet each day so it pays to be very selective. Typically a site will only keep postings for a few days before discarding it to make space for more recent postings.

In one sense the newsgroups are similar to email groups except that on Usenet the articles are stored once on the participating site's computer intead of by each user as would be the case in an email group.

Newsreaders

A newsreader is a program which enables you to read and post to Usenet. There are several but nn is one of the most popular. In many ways it is like an email program. It enables you to choose which newsgroups you subscribe to and to read and reply to postings which you have not yet seen.

An example of a screen when using nn is shown below. It is possible to post to newsgroups on Usenet using conventional email if you wish or by posting when in the newsreader. As for email, a subject is specified. There is an accepted etiquette about using Usenet. It is possible to restrict postings to geographical areas.

Open newsgroups often have a low signal to noise ratio. Some groups are moderated and postings are vetted and grouped before appearing. Such groups tend to have a higher signal to noise ratio.

World Wide Web

Also known as WWW, the Web and W3. Usenet contains dynamic and transient information, discussions, comment and news. The information is generally material you would read and discard.

By contrast WWW provides access to more durable information, reports, articles and information of almost every conceivable sort, including images, video, music and speech.

WWW is based on the idea of hypertext. Hypertext documents are electronic documents which contain embedded links to other parts of the information system. Imagine reading an article about trees. When specific trees are mentioned you may click on them and jump to further information on thoose particular trees, then return to where you were reading originally.

Hyperetext documents are non-linear i.e you dont read from start to finish. You navigate through, following links and back tracking to gain the information you require. Documents on the Web contain links to other documents which may be text, images, video clips, etc. Also, most importantly, the links may be to documents anywhere on the Internet. Also links need not simply be to static documents. or example, a link may take you into Usenet or initiate a telnet session.

The programs used to access the Web are called browsers. There are many different kinds. Browsers are clients in client/server systems. The Web sites providing information run Web servers which respond to messages from the client browsers. Some browsers only handle text. Others can handle the full range of multimedia information available from some Web sites on the net. Netscape has become one of the most common www browsers in the last two years.

The Web has become an attempt to organise all information on the iinternet as a set of hypertext documents. Its popularity is growing very rapidly indeed. Most universities, many companies and many other information providers are becoming Web sites. Even the White house has a web page with a sound clip from Bill Clinton.

The key to the usefulness of hypertext is in the hands of those who create the documents which are available on the Web; ie the uthors. Documents on the Web must be prepared using HTML (hypertext markup Language). HTML is a language for specifying the structure of documents, eg which parts are headings, which are paragraphs, images, lists etc and, most importantly, defining links. This involves associating the text from which you wish to make a link with the address of the document to which a user will be able to jump. The document to which the link is being made is specified by a URL, a universal resource locator. A URL may take the form: http://host/dir/subdir/filename.

Where host is the address of the computer containing the document and the rest is the pathname of the document required. http stands for hypertext transfer protocol and other protocols may be specified here if necessary. The browser uses this inormation to determine how to diplay the docuement.

Increasingly people are preparing documents in html. (eg in preference to using Latex or Word or whatever). Software for converting documents into html from other formats are beginning to appear but authors must add the link information which can be equally time consuming.

Although Usenet provides news and discussion, both can be handled via the Web as well. In general, Web information is more long lasting and involves more thought when authoring. Creating the links and formatting the document can be a non-trivial task. It is relatively easy to make standard text available on the Web without links; ie as destination anchors as opposed to source anchors.

Hypermedia Systems

Hypertext systems are information systems which handle the storing and structuring, the access and presentation of information. They allow users to navigate through the information in a non linear fashion by following links from one point in the information space to another point. Thus, unlike a book, a hypertext "document" is not sequential. It may contain links to other parts of the same document or to other documents and a user may jump around in the information, backtracking as necessary to the points from which jumps were made, to follow an earlier thread.

The term hypertext was coined by Ted Nelson in 1965 when he began to design Xanadu, a networked hypertext system. It is useful to distinguish between two classes of hypertext system: open and closed. Typically, a closed hypertext system embeds the information about links in the document files themselves using a special language such as html. The documents must be specially prepared for the closed hypertext system and it is not possible to author links to documents developed in other applications.

There is a major difference between authoring documents in a closed system and using the system as an information user. The author must be familiar with the special facilities for authoring and embedding the links. Thus, the cost of authoring is high in closed systems. Closed systems tend to have a limited range of link types, mainly specific links from one fixed point in a document to another fixed point in a document.

By contrast, open hypertext systems do not impose a special mark up on the documents in the system. The documents may remain in their native format and the open hypertext system can be integrated with third party applications for creating or displaying documents. This means that documents do not have to be specially prepared for open systems.

There is no major distinction between authors and users in open systems. End users may author their own links as they see fit because the links are held separately from the documents. It is also easy to add functionality in open hypertext systems and a range of link types will typically be available. With open systems, different users may see different link bases for the same documents.

Hypertext systems allow a flexible associations between a wide range of documents but a general disadvantage is to do with the wide range of paths through the material. Users can become disoriented in the information space, not knowing exactly where they are or how they reached there.

Microcosm

Over the last five years, the Multimedia Research Group at Southampton University has developed Microcosm, an open architecture multimedia information system (MMIS), which is not only a valuable vehicle for MMIS research but also a versatile open hypermedia system in which all datafiles remain in the native format of the application that created them. All link information is held in separate link databases (linkbases).

Link authoring within hypermedia applications is an arduous and time consuming process. As the size and complexity of the hypermedia applications increase the number of links needed to relate the disparate sections of information (or documents) also increases. Authoring every link by hand soon ceases to be feasible and Microcosm provides two powerful alternatives to the manual creation of every link. These are:

— *Generic links*: A generic link, once authored from a particular object (eg a text string), may be followed from any instance of the object at any location in any document. For example, one generic link could be authored from the text string *Southampton* to a video of the city. Wherever this string occurs in any document, the user can then follow the link to the video.

— *Compute Links:* Text documents within the application may be pre-indexed to allow full text retrieval searches. This is integrated into the link following environment so that the user can then select any piece of text and ask the system to attempt to provide related information according to a predefined algorithm. The facility is called compute links as it allows users to navigate through the information without following predefined links.

There is no doubt that both of the above mechanisms reduce the authoring load associated with the creation of large complex hypermedia applications. The former provides a method for replacing multiple links to the same destination with a single generic link and the latter provides a tool for relating documents without needing any links to be authored. However, until recently, these two mechanisms for reducing authoring load were only available for text. In the next section we provide an overview of recent extensions to the Microcosm architecture producing MAVIS (Microcosm Architecture for Video, Image and Sound) which allows authors to exploit the mechanisms for *generic links* and *compute links* on non-textual media.

Content Based Retrieval and Navigation

One of the major challenges for multimedia information systems (MMIS) developers is the provision of effective tools for navigating through, or retrieving images from image collections or other non-textual information such as video and sound sequences. Such tools lag a long way behind tools for handling text.

Confronted with a multimedia information system, with an image on the screen, we would like to be able to select the image or a sub-image and ask for other images or sub-images which are similar in some way to our particular selection.

If we can use the image content of the selection to match in some way with images or sub-images in the

MMIS, this is referred to as content based retrieval (CBR). Similarly, asking for other information relating to the image selection and navigating to that information using the content of the selection as the key, is referred to as content based navigation (CBN).

As an example, consider a user of an on-line multimedia furniture catalogue who finds a picture of a pine table in the catalogue and wishes to know if there are other items of furniture which might match the table in that or other manufacturers' catalogues. The user asks the computer to locate any similar images.

The system responds with all the other pieces of pine furniture of which it has knowledge. This process is CBR. The user then asks for more information about a specific item such as the price, the delivery date or a video of a house interior with the furniture in place. This process is CBN.

Retrieval and navigation with images in MMIS has been tackled for many years by the use of associated and manually assigned keys or the use of manually authored point to point links. By contrast, techniques which capitalise on the direct use of image content as an aid to navigation or retrieval are in their infancy. Research which can contribute to progress in this area comes not only from the multimedia community, but also from image database research and research into image understanding and computer vision

Published work includes descriptions of image databases which use a range of image properties for direct content based retrieval. Typically they are for use in specific application domains Some systems provide content based image retrieval tools of wider applicability but are often less powerful than those tuned to a specific application domain e.g. the QBIC (Query By Image Content) system developed by IBM.

Although these, and other projects address the problem of image retrieval by content either with or without semantic considerations, few papers have explicitly addressed the problem of content based retrieval within an MMIS environment and fewer have addressed the general issue of content based navigation through an MMIS. One exception is the Miyabi system under development at NEC, which is a hypermedia system in which non-textual information may be retrieved using queries presented in the same form as the medium to be retrieved.

In spite of significant progress in content based retrieval, it is clear that to achieve truly robust and versatile retrieval of images based on content will require a general solution to the recognition problem in image analysis and this is far from being achieved. However, parameterisations of shape, colour, texture and other image features can provide useful content cues for direct addressing of images and provide valuable filters for image matching and retrieval.

In the standard version of Microcosm, links are authored by selecting areas of documents to act as start and end anchors of the link and then choosing a create link action. The linking process within Microcosm then allows the author to select the type of link that they wish to create such as a generic link or button.

Links from text documents contain the selection that constitutes the link's start anchor. However, links from non-textual media do not. For example, a link from an image will contain the bounding box describing the selected area but not its content. Although this allows specific links from one place in a particular image, the lack of content means that generic links from non-textual material were not possible.

In MAVIS the architecture has been extended to allow links from non-textual media to include the content of their source anchors. This extension gives the system the potential to exploit generic links in non-text documents. The extension takes the form of a framework containing a collection of modules. Unlike text where the only comparison used to retrieve links is a straight forward string match, richer media such as images require many different matching algorithms.

Each module in the framework is responsible for maintaining everything needed to produce and maintain indexed representations, ie feature vectors representing the the content from the link start anchors for one matching process. For example, images can be matched using such features as colour distribution, shape and texture. Each feature is handled by a separate module in the framework.

The module maintains the data (processed representations of the link start anchor content) an index for the feature and an algorithm for matching features and generating similarity indices.

Navigation (CBN)

In the new system, when an author creates a link from an image, the selected source anchor area is processed to extract a representation(feature vector) of the chosen region. The representation is stored in an index together with the information about the other end of the link (the destination anchor).

In order to follow a link, the user selects an area of an image (in any document in the system) and the selected area is processed to obtain the feature vectors. These are then compared with the lists of feature vectors produced during the authoring stage. If a match or several matches are found (ie the feature vector is similar to one for which there is a link), the user may follow the corresponding links. A list of the best matches is displayed.

Retrieval (CBR)

Content based retrieval is the equivalent of full text retrieval but for non-text documents. Pre-indexing of the document using specific aspects of its content takes place. For example, an image may be indexed on colour distribution or object shape, whereas a sound document may be indexed using parameterisations of its constituent frequencies.

The MAVIS extensions include a framework for CBR from non-textual documents, in addition to the generic link facilities described above. The facility uses the same modules as those for generic link operation but without the need for manual creation of relations between regions of the documents. Instead, feature selections from the documents are used to generate the link entries, and any matches found will return the document corresponding to the match.

2

Technological Analysis

This chapter examines how unstated, but critical, assumptions which underlie social analyses of computerization frame our understanding. We will focus on the popular, professional and scholarly literature in which authors claim to describe the actual nature of computerization, the character of computer use, and the social choices and changes that result from computerization. Every year thousands of articles and dozens of books comment on the meaning of new computer technologies for people, organizations, and the larger society. Since computer technologies are likely to improve significantly over the next few decades, we should expect periodic accounts of the social meanings of new technologies. Moreover, as we approach the year 2000, there will be a predictable flood of books and articles that examine the virtues and problems of computer technology in the 21st century.

A large fraction of the literature about computing describes emerging technologies and the ways they can expand the limits of the possible. Faster, tinier computers can make it easier for people to access information in a wider variety of places. Larger memories can make more data accessible. Richer display devices can help people communicate more readily with computerized systems through pictures and text. High speed networks, such as Usenet and Internet, link thousands of computer systems together in ways only dreamed of in 1970.

The remarkable improvement in the capabilities of equipment from one decade to the next generate breathless excitement by researchers, developers, and entrepreneurs, as well as by the battalions of journalists who document these events in the daily newspapers and weekly magazines. Accounts of the powerful information processing capabilities of computer systems are usually central to many stories of computerization and social change. Authors write about these changes in technology and social life with different analytical and rhetorical strategies.

Some authors enchant us with images of new technologies that offer exciting possibilities of manipulating large amounts of information rapidly with little effort — to enhance control, to create insights, to search for information, and to facilitate cooperative work between people. Much less frequently, some authors examine a darker social vision in that any likely form of computerization will amplify human misery — people sacrificing their freedom to businesses and government agencies, people becoming very dependent on complex technologies that they don't comprehend, and sometimes the image of inadvertent global thermonuclear war. Both kinds of stories often reflect the conventions of utopian and anti-utopian writing.

Authors craft utopian and anti-utopian writings within a set of conventions that limit what they can or will say. Even though these writings talk about social forms that the authors suggest are likely, their tacit conventions preclude their discussing important social relationships that are also likely. A genre refers to any body of work that is characterized by a set of conventions. The works that we readily identify as Romantic comedies, impressionist paintings, horror films, newspaper editorials, and popular movie reviews are often constructed with a set of conventions that make them readily intelligible and accessible.

Authors and artists who work wholly within the conventions of a genre also limit the kinds of themes that they can effectively examine. Authors of romantic comedies usually have trouble exploring boredom in life and the ways that people work out sustained negotiations to get by day to day. Scholars have examined the ways that literary formulas shape fiction, journalistic conventions shape newsmaking, and academic conventions shape scholarship.

This chapter carries these conceptions of genre formulas as epistemological envelopes further into the realm of writing which is putatively non-fictional, writing which authors position as telling us truths about the world of computerization "out there" and beyond the author's imagination. A major theme of this chapter is that many social analyses of computing are written with genre conventions that limit the kinds of ideas that can be readily examined. Conventions make works more easily intelligible. A major contribution of this chapter is to examine some key genres of writing about computerization and to examine their conventions.

The utopian and anti-utopian genres of social analysis are about 500 years old, and predate the social sciences by about 350 years. Authors who work within these genres examine certain kind of social possibilities, and usually move quite freely beyond the technologies one finds in use today and beyond social relationships that are commonplace today.

Utopian tales are devised to stimulate hope in future possibilities, while anti-utopian tales are devised to stimulate anger at horrible possibilities. Technological utopianism is particularly influential in North America. Appreciating its epistemology helps understand an important aspect of North American thought. A different kind of investigative strategy and genres of reporting one's insights are based on examining existing computerized systems as they are actually used in real social settings.

These investigations and genres of writing that communicate them rest on the empiricist's faith that by examining the world as it is, we can learn something important of the worlds that might be. We will examine three major genres that rest on empirical observation: social realism, social theory, and analytical reduction. These are not the only genres of social analysis of computing. One can find works written with other conventions, such as expert surveys and personal reminiscences. But some of these five genres are commonplace, and others are important for developing systematic analyses.

Technological Utopianism

Utopian thinkers portray societies in which people live

ideal lives. The first such description appeared in Plato's Republic written some 2500 years ago. But the name Utopia derives from Thomas More, who published a story of an ideal society named Utopia in 1516. In Utopia people lived harmoniously and free of privation. His fanciful name, which meant "nowhere," has been picked up and applied to a whole tradition of writing and thinking about the forms of society that would make many people happiest. There have been hundreds of utopian blueprints. They differ substantially in their details: some have focused on material abundance as the key to human happiness while other have advanced visions of happiness based on austere and simple ways of life. Some utopians advocate private property as a central social institution, while many place a primacy on shared property.

The most obvious utopian sources are discourses which the authors identify as fictional accounts with traditional devices such as made up characters and fanciful dialogue. We are concerned with discourses about computerization which authors present as primarily realistic or factual accounts (and which are cataloged as non-fiction in bookstores and libraries). We will show how some these discourses are shaped by the conventions of utopianism and anti-utopianism.

Edward Feigenbaum and Pamela McCorduck explicitly identify with utopian ideals when they close their book about the social virtues of expert systems with this observation:

> ... "utopian" also means something we have said many times and in many ways that we desire as a human good.... all this ... corresponds to Adam Smith's vision in The Wealth of Nations of a

> universal opulent society, a condition of plenty that frees the people from dependence and subordination to exercise true independence of spirit in autonomous actions.

The British author Tom Stonier also illustrates the utopian tradition in writing about information technology. He ends his book about the way that information technologies can transform societies with this observation:

> To sum up, everyone an aristocrat, everyone a philosopher. A massively expanded education system to provide not only training and information about how to make a living, but also on how to live. In late industrial society, we stopped worrying about food. In late communicative society, we will stop worrying about material resources. And just as the industrial economy eliminated slavery, famine, and pestilence, so will the post-industrial economy eliminate authoritarianism, war, and strife. For the first time in history, the rate at which we will solve problems will exceed the rate at which they will appear. This will leave us to get on with the real business of the next century. To take care of each other. To fathom what it means to be human. To explore intelligence. To move out into space.

Utopian images are common in many books and articles about computerization in society written by technologists and journalists. We are particularly interested in what can be learned, and how we can be misled, by a particular brand of utopian thought — technological utopianism. This line of analysis places the use of some specific technology, such as computers, nuclear energy, or low-energy low-impact technologies, as key enabling elements of a utopian vision. Sometimes people will casually refer to exotic technologies — like pocket computers which understand spoken language — as "utopian gadgets." Technological utopianism does not refer to these technologies with amazing capabilities. It refers to analyses in which the use of specific technologies plays a key role in shaping a benign social vision. In contrast, technological anti- utopianism examines how certain broad families of technology are key enablers of a harsher and more destructive social order.

Technologists who characterize new or future technologies often rest on utopian imagery when they examine their social meanings or implications. In 1948, before there were any working electronic computers, Vannevar Bush set forth a vision of a fast, flexible, remotely accessible desk-sized computer, called "memex" which would allow a researcher to electronically search through vast archives of articles, books, and notes electronically. He wrote:

> Wholly new forms of encyclopedia will appear, ready-made with a mesh of associative trails running through them, ready to be dropped into the memex, and there amplified. The lawyer has at his touch the associated opinions and decisions of his whole experience. The patent attorney has on call millions of issued patents, with familiar trails to every point of his client's interest. The physician, puzzled by a patient's reaction, strikes the trail established in studying an earlier similar case, and runs rapidly through analogous case histories, with side references to the classics for the pertinent anatomy and histology. The chemist, struggling with the synthesis of an organic compound, has all the chemical literature before him in his laboratory, with trails following the analogies of compounds, the side trails to their physical and chemical behavior.

The historian, with a vast chronological account of people, parallels it with a skip trail which stops only at the salient items, and can follow at any time, contemporary trails which lead him all over civilization at a particular epoch. There is a new profession of trail blazers, those who find delight in the task of establishing useful trails through the enormous mass of the common record. The inheritance from the master becomes not only his additions to the world's record, but for his disciples, the entire scaffolding by which they were erected.

Thus science may implement the ways in which man produces, stores, and consults the records of the race.

Bush continued by describing the ways in which the users' ability to associate items, gather together the useful clusters of information that showed up during the search, and "instantly" project any or all of them onto displays for selective review, fast or slow.

Presumably, man's spirit should be elevated if he can better review his shady past and analyze more completely and objectively his present problems.

Bush envisioned a flexible, compliant research assistant able to artfully fish through vast archives of textual information and gather the useful stuff embodied in an uncomplaining ever-ready machine. A seductive image indeed! This vision was ever more remarkable because the image of digital computers that dominated scientific writing at the time — and even dominates scientific thinking in today's talk about supercomputers — was high speed calculation of numerical data.

We could have examined any number of other technological visions — of computer based instruction to transform education, or of information systems which would enable managers to more tightly control their business enterprises, etc. In part, these visions, like Bush's, rest on descriptions of computer-based devices and their information processing capabilities. In Fifth Generation, Edward Feigenbaum and Pamela McCorduck speculate about several possible applications of artificial intelligence to medicine, library searches, life at home, and help for the elderly.

Feigenbaum and McCorduck speculate in terms similar to Bush — by describing how these technologies might work under ideal conditions to help a person carry out socially useful actions. But they ignore key social conditions under which these technologies would be likely to be used. A remarkably talented engineer, Douglas Engelbart, was inspired by Bush's vision. About 15 years later, he assembled a brilliant research team at the Stanford Research Institute to build computer systems which resembled Bush's Memex.

At the time, computer technology had advanced to the point where room-sized computers could be "time-shared" by dozens of people and accessed through video displays in their offices. Engelbart described his project "to augment human intellect" in these terms: By 'augmenting human intellect' we mean increasing the capability of a man to approach a complex problem situation, gain comprehension to suit his particular needs, and to derive solutions to his problems.... we include the professional problems of diplomats, executives, social scientists, life scientists, physical scientists, attorneys, designers .... We refer to a way of life in an integrated domain where hunches, cut-and-try, intangibles, and the human 'feel for the situation' usefully coexist with powerful concepts, streamlined terminology and notation, sophisticated methods, and high powered electronic aids."

Engelbart's team designed a novel system which included technologies which began to appear in the marketplace in the mid-1980s, such as the mouse, hypertext, and context-sensitive help available with function keys. Engelbart's team focussed on computer systems which would enhance the performance of groups of people working together. They developed text systems which allowed different group members to have their own views of the same body of text. They built an electronic mail system which enabled people to track messages sent about various topics within their group.

There are some commercial "groupware" systems to facilitate the functioning of groups by allowing many people to work with common bodies of text, schedules, etc. Visions like Bush's and Engelbart's, from which we have drawn tiny excerpts, serve as an inspiration for many technologists and affectionados of new technologies. Visions like Bush's and Engelbart's are also flawed in the way they characterize technologies, people, and social life. They emphasize the ways that a technology should work ideally, under conditions where all the participants are highly cooperative to make things work their best. Some people call the field which researches and develops computer systems to support groups activities "computer supported cooperative work (CSCW)." In this label, the work of groups is implied to be cooperative by definition. Other kinds of social relationships in work groups — such as those marked by conflict, competition, coercion, and even combat, are denied to exist by definition.

In an illustrative review of software, Frank Derfler Jr. argued that group scheduling or calendaring software was a critical module of "workgroup productivity software," although other modules, such as text processing and electronic mail, are important to make a more usable system. Derfler goes on to say:

Scheduling three or more busy people for a meeting, along with arranging for a conference room and a slide projector, can be a frustrating and time-consuming task, requiring at least three phone calls. If one person or facility isn't available at the time the other people or facilities are, a whole series of negotiations begins. Mathematicians refer to it as progressive approximation; you (or your secretary making the arrangements) call it frustration. Before the scheduling problem is resolved, the number of people involved and phone calls made may have increased dramatically.

Scheduling programs ... vary in how they confirm proposed events. The simpler packages assume that if the event fits on the calendar, that the people scheduled to attend will be there. Other programs ask for confirmation, while some go as far as to tie into electronic mail modules for notification.

.... The best scheduling software is utterly useless if people aren't willing to play the game by keeping their personal calendars current. Obviously, these personal calendars are at the heart of the group scheduling process— calendars that aren't readily available or easy to use will never be maintained by group participants. With this in mind, it seems imperative that these programs allow you to run the personal calendar module (interactively while running other programs) and make it easy to use.

Derfler describes and critically evaluates key features of some major programs, and describes the best of these packages as dreams come true for busy professionals and managers. Like Vannevar Bush, Feigenbaum and McCorduck, he describes how these programs can facilitate various kids of group activities, such as scheduling, under the best of conditions: machines are up and running properly; people have immediate access to the shared system to keep their calendars up-to-date; people actually keep their calendars up-to-date. Unfortunately, like many journalists, he does not explain what social conditions make these packages most effective — or even usable at all.

Derfler's article is titled "Imposing Efficiency," but he never describes why or how efficiency would be imposed by anyone involved with the systems he reviews. In discussing meeting scheduling, he observes, "The best scheduling software is utterly useless if people aren't willing to play the game by keeping their personal calendars current." However, he immediately moves from this central observation to a technical point: that the scheduling software should be designed so that it can "pop-up" whenever a person is running some other application. That way, if a person schedules a meeting by telephone when she is doing something else, like writing a memo, she can promptly update her electronic calendars with a minimum of interruption. That's a valid point. But Derfler never goes beyond the technical observation to examine the social practices of "imposed efficiencies," specifically the requirement that users accept and cooperate with the demands of managers who are trying to improve productivity through computerized systems.

So far, our examples focus on computer-based systems used by relatively small groups. But powerful images that link computerization and larger scale social change have entered ordinary language through newspapers, popular books, and advertisements. Terms like "computer revolution," "information society," "knowledge worker," "computer-mediated work," "intelligent machine". These catch phrases have strong metaphorical associations. They are often introduced by authors to advance positive exciting images of computerization.

These new terms are often worked into common usage by journalists and authors who write for popular audiences. We live in a period of tremendous social changes. And sometimes new terms can help better capture emerging social patterns or new kinds of technologies, than can our conventional language. But the way that many authors casually use these terms often reflects important unexamined and often questionable social assumptions. Alvin Toffler helped stimulate enthusiasm for computerization in these popular terms in his best seller The Third Wave. He characterized major social transformations in terms of large shifts in the organization of society — driven by technological change.

The "Second Wave" was the shift from agricultural societies to industrial societies. He contrasts industrial ways of organizing societies with new social trends that he links to computer and microelectronic technologies. Toffler is masterful in succinctly suggesting major social changes in succinct breathless prose. He also invented some of his own terminology to help characterize key social changes — terms like second wave, third wave, electronic cottage, infosphere, technosphere, prosumer, intelligent environment, etc. Many of his new terms did not become commonly accepted. Even so, they help frame a seductive description of social change, as this excerpt from his chapter, "The Intelligent Environment" illustrates his approach:

Today, as we construct a new info-sphere for a Third Wave civilization, we are imparting to the "dead" environment around us, not life, but intelligence. A key to this revolutionary advance is of course, the computer.

As miniaturization advanced with lightening rapidity, as computer capacity soared and prices per function plunged, small cheap powerful minicomputers began to sprout everywhere. Every branch factory, laboratory, sales office, or engineering department claimed its own.... The brainpower of the computer ... was "distributed." This dispersion of computer intelligence is now moving ahead at high speed.

The dispersal of computers in the home, not to mention their interconnection in ramified networks, represents another advance in the construction of an intelligent environment. Yet even this is not all. The spread of machine intelligence reaches another level altogether with the arrival of microprocessors and microcomputers, those tiny chips of congealed intelligence that are about to become a part, it seems, of nearly all the things we make and use.

What is inescapably clear, however, whatever we choose to believe, is that we are altering our info-sphere fundamentally.... we are adding a whole new strata of communication to the social system. The emerging Third Wave info-sphere makes that of the Second Wave era - dominated by its mass media, the post office, and the telephone - seem hopelessly primitive by contrast.

In all previous societies, the infosphere provided the means for communication between human beings. The Third Wave multiplies these means. But it also provides powerful facilities, for the first time in history, for machine-to-machine communication, and, even more astonishing, for conversation between humans and the intelligent environment around them. When we stand back and look at the larger picture, it becomes clear that the revolution in the info-sphere is at least as dramatic as that of the technosphere — in the energy system and the technological base of society. The work of constructing a new civilization is racing forward on many levels at once.

Toffler's breathless enthusiasm can be contagious — but also stymies critical thought. Like Derfler, he assumes that key people — e.g., administrators and purchasing agents — will share his enthusiasm for the new technologies. Toffler also ignores cost constraints. Today, for example, many small colleges and universities are unable to provide adequate computer support for their faculty and students; community groups and poorer organizations also have trouble affording adequate computer systems. Toffler illustrated changes in the infosphere with, The Source, a large commercial US-based computer-communication and messaging system which has thousands of individual and corporate subscribers.

Today, he could multiply that example manifold with the emergence of competing commercial systems in the US, such as Compuserve, Prodigy and Genie, as well as tens of thousands of individually owned computerized bulletin boards that people have set up in hundreds of cities and towns. Similarly one could ask about the social roles of other messaging systems, such as Minitel which supports numerous sexy messageries. However, there have been a myriad of other changes in the information environment in the United States which are not quite as exciting to people who would like to see a more thoughtful culture. For example, television has become a major source of information about world events for many children and adults. The popular television shows include soap operas, sitcoms, and rock video television networks like MTV.

Television news, the most popular "factual" kind of television programming, slices stories into salami-thin 30-90 second segments and fits them to simple storylines. Moreover, there is some evidence that functional illiteracy is rising in the United States. The problems of literacy in the United States are probably not only a byproduct of television's popularity. But it is hard to take Toffler's optimistic account seriously when a large fraction of the population has trouble understanding key parts of the instruction manuals for automobiles and for commonplace home appliances, like refrigerators and televisions.

Toffler opens up important questions about the way that information technologies alter the ways that people perceive information, the kinds of information they can get easily, and how they handle the information they get. But his account — like many popular accounts — caricatures the answers by using only illustrations which support his generally buoyant theses. And he skillfully sidesteps tough questions while creating excitement (such as, "The work of constructing a new civilization is racing forward on many levels at once.").

Toffler's vision is not dated, however. Ten years later two respected information systems scholars examined offices of the late 1990s:

"The office of the late 1990s can now be envisioned. Its staff of professionals and managers are surrounded by intelligent devices that speak, listen, or interact with them to determine what is to be accomplished and how it is to be done. Contacts with other departments, other divisions, customers, vendors, and other organizations are made with little effort and without human intervention. Behind the scenes, systems are being developed by system developers equipped with versatile and highly integrated software."

This vision is similar to Toffler's, but less poetic. It portrays computerized information systems and offices similar to a spaceship in which the crew is highly automated and staffed with robots.

In a similarly upbeat manner, John Sculley, former Chairman of the Board of the Apple Computer Corporation, advocates the development of simulation, hypermedia and artificial intelligence to strengthen the United States economy and educational systems. He argued by analogy with the role of print in the Renaissance. Sculley claims that print technology catalyzed the Renaissance which broke the stranglehold of the church and feudal interests on the population of Europe. He argues that computer systems based on hypermedia, simulation, and artificial intelligence applied to education are the appropriate means for a similar transformation today. Sculley's article is typical of some which try to excite a positive sense of purpose for developers and users of new computer technologies by referring to big historical changes such as the Renaissance or the Industrial Revolution. They excite hope for computerization by linking it to positive social ideals which they anchor in oversimplified and sometimes distorted historical accounts.

Technological utopianism because it is a common genre for exploring the social meaning of new and future technologies in North America. And it is the genre which is most influential in the North American technological communities.

Technological Anti-Utopianism

There is a relatively small North American literature which critically examines key claims made about the social virtues of different computerization strategies. The technological anti-utopian critiques portray computerization —in almost any form the analyst can conceive — as likely to degrade social life. They amplifies the underside of every computerized system which he discusses. For example, they criticizes visions of computerized databases which record historical data, because they usually eliminate important information which is too complex or costly to include.

The computer has thus begun to be an instrument for the destruction of history. For when society legitimates only those "data" that are in one standard format, then history, memory itself, is annihilated. *The New York Times* has already begun to build a "data bank" of current events. Of course, only those data that are easily derivable as by-products of typesetting machines are admissible to the system.

As the number of subscribers to this system grows, as they learn to rely more and more upon "all the news that was once fit to print," as *The Times* proudly identifies its editorial policy, how long will it be before what counts as fact is determined by the system, before all other knowledge, all memory, is simply declared illegitimate? Soon a supersystem will be built, based on the New York Times' data bank (or one very much like it), from which "historians" will make inferences about what "really" happened, about who is connected to whom, and about the "real" logic of events.

Weizenbaum's observations gain more force when one realizes that journalists don't simply report "the facts." They often rely upon standard kinds of sources, voices of publicly legitimate authority, in framing stories. For example, when a university alters a curriculum, deans and professors are more likely to have a voice in the resulting news story than are students. Gaye Tuchman characterized reporters in search of a story as casting a selective "newsnet" around their favorite kinds of sources. Journalists rarely cast their nets to give equal voice to all kinds of informed parties. While reporters are much more likely to go to "the grass roots" today than they were in the days of Vannevar Bush, each newspaper prints a mix of stories in a style which reflects a relatively stable character.

Usually, even if the mastheads were interchanged, one would not confuse the New York Times with a small town weekly newspaper. Without special design, nothing in the database technology would be likely to give a user a clue about its real limitations in representing a narrow range of perspectives. And, yet, its convenience might make it very tempting for a busy professional to rely on it as a primary source, without appreciating its limitations. That is the cautionary note that one might draw from Weizenbaum's bitter observations. But Weizenbaum's argument is primarily polemical. He doesn't discuss any virtues of news databases or conditions under which they might not have the deleterious problems he identifies. News databases can also substantially assist in useful research as long as they do not become a sole source of information. Professional historians who have developed strong criteria for verifying events with original sources may be less likely to become their prisoners than many professionals (and students) who find them efficacious and seductive, despite their limitations. Moreover, Weizenbaum speaks with authority about future events ("soon a supersystem will be built...")

Discussions of computerization and work have been a major topic for both utopian and anti-utopian analysts. Some authors argue that computerization has systematically degraded clerical work through a pattern of industrialization. Some go farther and argue that the computerization of clerical work sets the stage for the industrialization of professional work as well. Mowshowitz summarizes his sharp vision in these concise terms:

> Our principal point is that the lessons of the factory are the guiding principles of office automation. In large offices, clerical work has already been transformed into factory-like production systems. The latest technology — office automation — is simply being used to consolidate and further a well-established trend. For most clerical workers, this spells an intensification of factory discipline. For many professionals and managers, it signals a gradual loss of autonomy, task fragmentation and closer supervision — courtesy of computerized monitoring. Communication and interaction will increasingly be mediated by computer. Work will become more abstract ... and opportunities for direct social interaction will diminish.

Like Weizenbaum, Mowshowitz writes authoritatively about distressing future events. He doesn't examine the possibility that many professionals will use their occupational power to resist the loss of autonomy and fragmented jobs that he describes. Nor does he examine how some professionals have exploited computerization to their advantage — in making their jobs more interesting and complex. Elsewhere in his article, he criticizes studies which examine such variations as concerned with "minutiae." Mowshowitz follows Braverman's line of argument that (under capitalism), managers will computerize so as to enhance their control by degrading working conditions. Braverman's thesis has been subject to significant discussion and found wanting, because it doesn't account for other processes that shape computerization (such as enhancing control over expensive resources other than labor or improving product quality in the face of competition).

Braverman's thesis is anti-utopian insofar as only one tragic outcome is likely. It is an important line of argument insofar as it locates computerization efforts within a logic of managerial interests, and highlights the importance of controlling labor as a key managerial interest. Utopian and anti-utopian analysts share important common conventions. Their narratives are usually future oriented, universalize experiences with technologies, homogenize experiences into one or two groups, and portray technologies as totalizing elements which dominate important social interactions.

They take extreme, but different, value positions. They portray computerization with monochromatic brushes: white or black. The technological anti-utopians' characterizations of the tragic possibilities of computerization provide an essential counterbalance to the giddy-headed optimism of the technological utopian accounts. The romances and tragedies are not all identical. For example, some anti- utopian writings examine the possibilities of computerized systems for coercion, while others emphasize alienation. But the technological utopian and anti-utopian genres have some important inherent limitations which we now examine.

Questions about the social consequences of new technologies are central to choices about paths for development, levels of social investment, and regulatory policies. These all merit analysis to help us better understand future possibilities. All such analyses rest on theories of the interplay between technological developments and social life. Utopian and anti-utopian themes are the most common in this culture.

Utopian visions are sometimes characterized as "reality transcending". They play important roles in stimulating hope and giving people a positive sense of direction. But they can mislead when their architects exaggerate the likelihood of easy and desirable social changes. Writing about technological utopianism in the 1930s, Wilson, Pilgrim and Tasjian comment:

> Belief in the limitless future potential of the machine had both its positive and negative aspects. During the 1930s this almost blind faith in the power of the machine to make the world a better place helped hold a badly shattered nation together. ... These science fiction fantasies contributed to an almost naive approach to serious problems and a denial of problems that could already be foreseen.

Anti-utopian writings are far less numerous in the United States. They serve as an important counterbalance to technological utopianism. But they could encourage a comparably ineffective sense of despair and inaction. Utopian and anti- utopian visions embody extreme assumptions about technology and human behavior. But their causal simplicity gives them great clarity and makes them easy to grasp — to enjoy or to abhor. They can resonate with our dreams or nightmares. Consequently, they have immense influence in shaping the discussions (and real directions) of computerization.

Technological utopian analysts portray a world which is free of substantial conflict. Technological anti-utopians usually portray certain fundamental conflicts such as between social classes or between government agencies and the public as almost unalterably unbalanced. One side virtually dominates while the other side mounts negligible resistance. Neither extreme characterizes the world in which social conflicts are important but in which coalitions draw complex lines and the intensity of conflict varies in place and time. Practical attempts to establish utopian social schemes have been fraught with significant and complex conflicts. For example, the United States was founded premises that were utopian in the 1700s.

The Declaration of Independence asserts that "all men were created equal" and that they would be should be guaranteed the right to "life, liberty, and the pursuit of happiness." This was in significant contrast to the political cultures of the European monarchies of the time, where the rule of the king or queen, and nobles, most of whom were selected by heredity, determined peoples' fates. Of course, asserting this right as universal didn't immediately make it so. Utopian ideals are hard to realize. Their advocates often have to fight hard to change social practices to better fit their ideals. Bloody revolutions were fought in the United States and France to overthrow the ruling monarchies in the late 18th centuries. Almost 200 years later, Martin Luther King and others advanced the cause of improved civil rights in the United States through aggressive confrontations: marches, rallies, court injunctions and sit ins, as well as through more quite persuasion. These social changes which altered the balance of privilege and exploitation did not come quietly and peacefully.

Distribution of Knowledge

In utopian analyses of computerization, people have whatever skills they need to adequately use systems and to resolve problems as they arise. Anti-utopian analyses vary in their accounts of technological skills. Sometimes everyone is adequately skilled, but are using technologies in ways that undermine important social values. In other anti-utopian accounts, many people are confused about key social relationships and the use of technologies. In these latter analyses, either elites control key skills or sometimes no one has key knowledge (as in Weizenbaum's account of "incomprehensible systems."). These accounts rarely portray people's technological skills as being distributed in complex ways: many people as having adequate technical skills for some of their activities, and muddling through on others with help from co-workers or consultants, and being confused about a few technological activities.

Technological Development

Technological utopians sometimes recognize that new technologies cause new problems — but these are to be solved with additional technologies. Buckminster Fuller argued that it was difficult and almost pointless to teach people to drive very cautiously and to harass them with rigid laws. He argued for safer cars rather than for changing human behavior.

Today's discussions that focus on computerized "smart cars" rather than smart drivers runs along a parallel line. Technological utopians would usually advocate government funds invested in stimulating the development of new technologies rather than increasing the scale and scope of regulatory bureaucracies. As another kind of example, technological utopian discussions of computerization in schools emphasize the potentials of new technologies and ignore the ways that they may be unrealized when classes are overcrowded, teachers are not very sharp, and schools spend substantial efforts in trying to regiment students. By focussing on new technologies as agents of social change and assuming that social systems will use them effectively, technological utopians ignore the social conditions for technologies to be effective. Consequently, they often overstate their social value. In contrast, technological anti- utopians often understate the social value of technological innovations and the way that all technologies pose problems.

Necessity of Technological Effects

Technological utopian and anti-utopian analysts suggest that the changes they foresee are virtually certain to happen if a technology is developed and disseminated. Their arguments gain rhetorical force through linear logics and the absence of important contingencies. This causal simplification is, in our view, a fatal flaw of utopian and anti-utopian speculations. They explore the character of possible social changes as if they were the only likely social changes.

Not all technological utopian (or anti-utopian analyses) are equally coherent, clear, or credible. But other forms of social analysis can also be incoherent or baseless. So clarity does not differentiate between utopian analyses and other modes of social analysis. Attractive alternatives to utopian analysis should be more credible in characterizing conflict in a social order, the distribution of knowledge, the ways of solving problems that arise from new technologies, and resting upon less deterministic logics of social change.

Most important, they would also identify the social contingencies which make technologies (un)workable and social changes benign or harmful for various social groups. Analyses in these three genres often acknowledge complex patterns of social conflict, yet are more open-ended and contingent than both genres of utopian analysis.

Social Realism

"Social realism" to characterize a genre which uses empirical data to examine computerization as it is actually practiced and experienced. Social realists write their articles and books with a tacit label: But the genre is best characterized by the efforts of authors to communicate their understanding of computerization as it "really works" based on reporting fine grained empirical detail. Social realism gains its force through gritty observations about the social worlds in which computer systems will be used.

An interesting example of social realism is found in a study of instructional computing in classrooms by Sheingold, Hawkins and Char. They report on a number of ethnographic studies of instructional computing in specific classrooms, including the use of databases, a mathematical game, and LOGO programming. They carefully report different ways that teachers conceptualize the relationship between these programs and instruction (with resulting differences in ways that they integrate them into their classes).

They also report a variety of ways that students use the programs, from those that fit conventional rationalist conceptions of media in learning to those that simply get the work done. In some instances the students wrote and ran their programs as they were instructed to. They worked together so that they all participated in solving problems and also in entering programs into their computers. This division of labor between a girl who took control of the problem solving and her partner who handled the mechanics of transcribing the LOGO program illustrates the ways that people will organize so as to rapidly complete their work done, but not necessarily satisfy broader (utopian) educational goals. Another example of social realism is Grudin's analysis of the social assumptions that designers and advocates of groupware make about the use of these packages. He argues that the meeting scheduling systems championed by Derfler work best when their users all have secretaries to help keep their calendars up-to-date.

These packages are especially attractive to managers, who often have secretaries, and who often want to schedule meetings with subordinates. They can be a burden to professionals who do not have secretarial support. They can also burden people who are away from their desks in meetings out of their offices part of the day, where they are making new commitments which are not reflected in their shared calendars.

More deeply, Grudin examines computer applications with a model of organizations in which resources and authority are not equally distributed. Grudin places computer systems in work worlds in which there is a political economy of effort — some people can generate work for others. And the people who generate work may not have to work as hard as do the people who have to meet their requirements. Grudin's article examines the social contingencies which make these systems (un)workable. And Grudin takes some care in identifying which kinds of groupware are more troublesome. Social realists vary in the extent to which they weave their evidence into tight narratives. Tighter stories can leave us more satisfied. But there is a risk that important elements that don't fit the narrative are ignored.

More frequently social realism offers us compelling frank portraits which suffer from particularism. Authors in this genre rarely are explicit in drawing concepts or themes which generalize across technologies and social settings from the rich literature about the social character of computerization, or in contrasting their study with many other studies or accounts in the computerization literature. Moreover, it is always debatable what the present can tell us about what the future can be like if social arrangements or technologies are substantially transformed.

Social Theory

In contrast with social realism, theoretical analysts explicitly develop or test concepts and theories that transcend specific situations. Unlike utopian and anti-utopian accounts, social theoretical works are not "reality transcending." But they are situation transcending. Some examples are reinforcement politics, web models, structuration theory, post-structuralist theories, Judith Perrolle's explication of social control theories, and Terry Winograd's explication of language-action theory.

Web models illustrate this kind of theoretical work. Walsham, Symons and Waema characterize web models in these terms: "The basic tenet of web models is that a computer system is best conceptualized as an ensemble of equipment, applications and techniques with identifiable information processing capabilities. Each computing resource has costs and skill requirements which are only partially identifiable; in addition to its functional capabilities as an information processing tool it is a social object which may be highly charged with meaning.

There is no specially separable 'human factor' for information systems: the development and routine operations of computer-based technologies hinge on many human judgement and actions, often influenced by political interests, structural constraints, and participants' definition of their situations. The network of producers and consumers around the focal computing resource is termed the 'production lattice'; the interdependencies in this network form the 'web' from which the model derives its name. The production lattice is a social organization which is itself embedded in a larger matrix of social and economic relations ('macrostructure') and is dependent upon a local infrastructure. According to web models, these macrostructures and local infrastructures direct the kind of computer-based service available at each node of the production lattice, and since they evolve over time computing developments are shaped by a set of historical commitments. In short, web models view information systems as 'complex social objects constrained by their context, infrastructure and history'.

Web analyses are action-oriented and examine the political interplay of coalitions in structured — but somewhat fluid — settings. The main organizing concepts were a "focal computing technology" which was the center of analysis, the infrastructure which supported its development and operation (including production lattices), its context of development and use, and a history of organizational commitments which structured these arrangements. Researchers have applied web models to better understand a variety of cases, including dilemmas of developing the Worldwide Military Command and Control System, dilemmas of converting complex inventory control systems in manufacturing firms, the development of software in insurance firms, and the ways in which desktop computerization changes worklife in offices.

Social theoretical studies of computerization offer the traditional virtues of theory: relatively concise general explanations and concepts which help guide inquiry in new situations. But they are much less accessible to a broad audience than technological utopian, anti-utopian and social realist accounts because of their intellectual demands: their (necessary) use of specialized terms and their frequent abstraction from the kinds of concrete situations that readers can readily visualize and perhaps identify with. The contrast between social realism and social theory, as ideal types, is rather clear. And it is easy to find books and articles which illustrate these types. All social analyses are imbued with theoretical assumptions, however implicit. Journalists and others who are not trained in the social sciences are much more likely to write as social realists rather than as social theorists. Social scientists are more capable of developing theoretical inquiries, but they are more likely to publish social realist discourses about computerization or documents which apply existing theory to sharpen realist accounts.

Analytical Reduction

Some scholars organize their social investigations into computerization by working within a tightly defined conceptual framework. They identify a few key concepts, sometimes derived from theory or abstracted from a group of studies, and examine them in new settings. If they adopt a strictly quantitative social science approach, they operationalize all of their key concepts into variables, measure them, examine how behaviors are distributed along the variables and via mathematical relationships between variables (e.g., correlations). While completely quantitative studies represent ideal examples of this genre, studies which focus on a few qualitatively described dimensions share enough key characteristics to be appropriate to group with them also.

Hiltz's, on the ways that computer conferencing systems alter productivity of groups illustrates the quantitative version of the genre. Hiltz administered questionnaires to people who used four different computer conferencing system before and after a period of use. She grouped four survey questions items into a summary measure of productivity (e.g., quality of work with system, quantity of work with system, overall usefulness of system and utility of system in reaching other people). She measured many aspects of the groups, their work, their usage of the conferencing systems, and the features of the systems. She bases her conclusions on the magnitude of quantitative relationships between the variables which she measured. For example, she notes:

> The strongest correlates of productivity improvements for all four systems are pre-use expectations about whether the system would increase productivity. Other determinants relate to the group context: leadership skill is important and strong competitive feelings may hamper productivity.

The development of a complex computerized inventory control system could best be explained by one of three different kinds of organizational choices processes: rational decision making, organizational drift, and partisan politics. In this study we presented a qualitative case study, and then systematically examined it for evidence in the form of episodes and social relationships which would support or undermine each of these three models of organizational choice.

Depending on one's view, this approach represents the best or worst of social science inquiry. Those who see it as a valuable genre appreciate the way that the authors critically examine key concepts and examine the extent to which they shed insight into the social world of computing. They believe that our best hope for systematically understanding the social character of computerization will come from studies in this genre.

Those who criticize, or sometimes even despise analytical reduction, see it as arcane and inaccessible except to academic specialists. They usually prefer social realist studies because they are more easily accessible and identifiably concrete. Further, the quantitative reductions are less likely to characterize the shifts of understandings that participants have over time, the nature of unusual but important events, or even the occasions when computerization becomes comical or tragic.

3

Politics of Search Engines

Enhanced by the technology of the World Wide Web, internet has become an integral part of the ever-expanding global media system, moving into center stage of media politics alongside traditional broadcast media – television and radio. Enthusiasts of the "new medium" have heralded it as a democratizing force that will give voice to diverse social, economic and cultural groups, to members of society not frequently heard in the public sphere. It will empower the traditionally disempowered, giving them access both to typically unreachable nodes of power and previously inaccessible troves of information.

To scholars of traditional media, these optimistic claims must have a ring of familiarity, echoing similar optimistic predictions concerning the democratizing and empowering capacities of both radio and television. Instead of the expected public gains and fulfilment of democratic possibilities, instead of the spreading of access and power, however, the gains were consolidated in the hands of a few dominant individuals and institutions.

According to acclaimes media critic Robet McChesney the American media system is spinning out of control in a hyper-commercialized frenzy. Fewer than ten transnational media conglomerates dominate much of our media; fewer than two dozen account for the overwhelming majority of our newspapers, magazines, films, television, radio, and books.

With every aspect of our media culture now fair game for commercial exploitation, we can look forward to the full-scale commercialization of sports, arts, and education, the disappearance of notions of public service from public discourse, and the degeneration of journalism, political coverage, and children's programming under commercial pressure.

McChesney's works traces—in very subtle and convincing detail—how commercial interests were woven into the very fiber of the modern media networks through legislation, market mechanisms, and the like. These moves progressively pushed out and silenced the public service agenda, which was very central to the vision of the early pioneers in the field—McChesney's historical account of radio is very telling in this regard. His central argument, historically grounded, is that the fundamental course of media is determined primarily by how they're owned and operated.

Most US communication media—going back to AM radio in the 1920s—have followed this path: At first, when they do not seem commercially viable, they are developed by the nonprofit, noncommercial sector. When their profit-making potential emerges, however, the corporate sector start colonizing the media, and through a variety of mechanisms, usually its dominance of politicians, muscle out the rest and take over.

McChesney argues that this pattern is seen in the cases of FM radio, in UHF television, and to some extent in satellite and cable. On the prospects of the Internet, there are divergent predictions.

Some, like Dan Schiller and McChesney, influenced by their knowledge of other media, anticipate a similar narrowing of prospects for the Internet. They point to the commitment of the United States to private ownership of communications technology as the single most important and consistent historical policy position that influenced the course of telecommunications development.

And this same commitment is clearly evident in the rhetoric of the political foundations of the Internet, namely, the fact that of five 'values' that Vice-President Gore identified as ones that should define and guide the development of the GII, the first one listed was "private investment. Schiller asks, "What is the likelihood of robust adherence to...elemental democratic prescription, when the character of the network development is now all-too-evidently to be given mainly as a function of unrestrained corporate ambition and private design?.

Others, like Mark Poster, offer a contrasting view, arguing that the distinctly "post-modern" nature of the Internet, with its capacity to disseminate material rather than centralize it, will discourage the endowment of authority – both academic as well as political. Its development, therefore, is unlikely to mirror that of previous media.

The broader debate about the dual possibilities of media: to be democratizing or to be colonized by specialized interests at the expense of the public good, inspires and motivates this chapter on the politics of search engines. The general position we defend, and illustrate in this one case, is that although the Internet and the Web offer exciting prospects for furthering the public good, the benefits are conditional, resting precariously on a number of political, economic and technical factors. Following Poster, we are buoyed by clear instances where the Web and Internet have served broad political and ends. But we also see irrefutable signs of gradual centralization and commercialization of guiding forces. Like McChesney, we are particularly concerned with the way these competing interests may, early on, be woven in, or out, of the very fiber of media networks. Search engines constitute a particularly telling venue for this competition. And prospects, as seen from the perspective of the time of writing this chapter, do not look good for broad public interests.

Search engines constitute a powerful source of access and accessibility within the Web. Access, already a thorny issue, is the subject of much scholarship and research, as well as a lengthy report of the National Telecommunications and Information Administration (NTIA) Falling through the Net.

Focussing on social, economic and racial factors, these works show how access to the Web is preconfigured in subtle but politically important ways, resulting in exclusion of significant voices. It is not enough, however, to worry about overcoming these traditional barriers, to focus only on the granting of entry to the media space of the Web. It is not enough if, as we argue, the space itself is distorted in favor of those wealthy in technical or economic resources through the mechanism of biased search engines.

The politics of search engines thus represents the broader struggle to sustain the democratic potential of traditional media, the Internet, and the World Wide Web in particular. In a statistical study of Web search engines, S. Lawrence and C.L. Giles estimated that none of the search engines they studied, taken individually, index more than 16% of the total indexable Web, which they estimate to consist of 800 million pages. Combining the results of the search engines they studied, they estimated the coverage to increase to approximately 42%. This confirms the primitive impressions of many users, namely, that the Web is almost inconceivably large, and also that search engines only very partially meet the desperate need for an effective way of finding things.

When judging what the producers of search engines have accomplished so far, optimists, focusing on the half-full portion of the cup, may legitimately marvel at progress in Web search technologies and at the sheer bulk of pages that are successfully found. In this chapter, however, we are concerned with the half-empty portion of the cup: the portions of the Web that remain hidden from view.

The purpose of this chapter is not, however, to bemoan the general difficulties of building comprehensive search engines, nor to highlight the technological difficulties that must surely impose limits on the range of scope and coverage that even the best search engines can achieve. Our concern, rather, is with the ways that developers, designers and producers of search engines will direct these technological limitations, the influences that may come into play in determining any systematic inclusions and exclusions, the wide-ranging factors that dictate systematic prominence for some sites, dictating systematic invisibility for others. These, we think, are political issues. They are important because what people are able to find on the Web determines what the Web consists of for them.

Although a complete discussion of the technical detail of search engines is beyond the scope of this chapter, we highlight aspects of search engines that we consider relevant to our discussion of their politics. We briefly discuss the nature of the connection between search engines and Web pages, the process by which this relationship is established, and how this relationship affects the producers (or owners) of Web pages wishing to have their pages recognized. Web-page providers seeking recognition from search engines for their Web pages must focus on two key tasks:

a) being indexed and

b) achieving a ranking in the top 10-20 search results displayed.

On Being Indexed

Having a page indexed, the essential first stage of being recognized by search engines, is extremely important. Without much exaggeration one could say that to exist is to be indexed by a search engine. If a webpage is not in the index of a search engine, a person wishing to access it must know the complete URL —webpage address—such as http://is.lse.ac.uk/lucas/cepe98.html for the CEPE'98 conference.

Since there is no rigid standard for producing URLs they are not obvious or even logical, in the way we tend to think that the addresses of our physical homes are logical. Sometimes the Internet domain name structure may help, such as 'ac.uk' or 'edu' for an academic institution in the United Kingdom or United States. However, for most searches we do not have any idea of the URLs involved. This is where search engines enter the picture. They create a map of the Web by indexing webpages according to keywords, and then create enormous databases that link page content, to keywords, to URLs.

When a seeker of information submits a keyword (or phrase)—presumably, one that best captures her interest—the search engine database ideally returns to the seeker a list of URLs linked to that keyword, ideally including all those that are relevant to the seeker's interest.

It is important to note that search engines use the notion of a keyword (i.e. that which is indexed and hence used for searching) in a rather minimal sense. Keywords are not determined a priori by the designers of the search engines' databases, nor, explicitly, by some other authority, but rather they are "deduced" from Web pages themselves in the process of indexing.

In a particular Web page a keyword(s) can be any of the following:

— Actual keywords indicated by the Web page designer in an HTML metatag as follows:

  <meta NAME="keywords" CONTENT="list of keywords">

— All, or some of the words appearing in the title which is indicated by the HTML <TITLE> tag as follows:

  <TITLE>Whatever is the title of the page</TITLE>.

— The first X words in a Web page (possibly excluding stop words).

— All the words in the Web page (possibly excluding stop words).

Most search engines use at least some of the words in the title tag of the Web page as the relevant keywords for indexing purposes. It is obviously important for Web page producers as well as seekers to know what words on a particular Web page are 'seen' as keywords by the indexing software of search engines. Thus, one might naturally ask: How does a search engine go about creating its database and what does it store in it? The answer to this question depends on which of basically two categories (and within these categories, the further subcategories) the search engine fits.

One category includes directory-based search engines such as Yahoo! and Aliweb. In this category, the vast majority of the pages indexed are manually submitted to the search engines' editors by Webmasters (and other creators of Web pages). The other category includes search engines that automatically harvest URLs by means of spiders (also referred to as robots or softbots).

Among the most well-known search engines fitting this category are: Alta Vista, Lycos, and Hotbot. In the case of directory-based search engines, Web-page creators submit URLs to the search engines for possible inclusion into their databases. If you wanted your page recognized by Yahoo!, for example, you would submit your URL and background information to a human editor who would review the page(s) and decide whether or not to schedule your page for indexing.

If your page is scheduled for indexing, it would be retrieved by the indexing software, which would parse the page and index it according to the keywords (content) found in the page. For directory-based search engines, therefore, human gatekeepers hold the key to inclusion in their indexed databases. There is a considerable backlog so that this process can take up to six months from the time of submission to the time of inclusion.

Web owners wishing to have their pages indexed must surely wonder what criteria these human editors use to decide whether or not to index their pages? This is a major bone of contention, especially for anyone contesting these decision criteria. With Yahoo!, for example, representatives say that they use criteria of relevancy.

The exact nature of these criteria, however, is not widely known nor publicly disseminated and, evidently, these criteria are not consistently applied by the various editors. As a result you may have your page rejected and would not know what to do to get it accepted. Danny Sullivan, the editor of Search Engine Watch, believes that the base success rate for any submitted page being listed with Yahoo! is approximately 25%.

Two factors that seem to increase the chances of being listed are the number of links (to and from a given site—also referred to as inlinks and outlinks), and how full a particular category happens to be. Where editors feel they need more references within a category, they lower the entry barriers.

Defending their approach, representatives of Yahoo! maintain they list what users want, arguing that if users were not finding relevant information they would cease using Yahoo!. With Aliweb, a very small site when compared with its competitors, users submit supplemental information about their Web-page content and keywords, as a way to help the indexing software improve the quality of its indexing and hence provide better search results.

Representatives of Aliweb emphasize that they do not provide comprehensive coverage; rather, they emphasize high quality search results. Because this is a small site, it is still able to index most of its submissions. As it becomes larger, it may, like its competitors, need to establish criteria for inclusion and exclusion.

Being indexed by search engines that automatically harvest URLs is a matter of being visited by a spider. Spiders usually start crawling from a historical list of URLs, especially documents with many links elsewhere, such as server lists, "What's New" pages, and other popular sites on the web. Software robots "crawl" the Web—that is, automatically traverse the Web's hypertext structure—first retrieving a document, and then recursively retrieving all documents that are referenced (linked by other URLs) in the original document.

Web owners interested in having their pages indexed might wish they had access to the detail of routes that robots follow when they crawl, which sites they favor, which they visit and how often, which not, and so forth. This, however, is a complicated technical subject, which mostly is treated and steadfastly guarded as trade secrets by the respective search engine companies.

From our experience and discussion with those involved in the field we would contend with some certainty that robots are guided by a set of criteria that steer them in a systematic way to select certain types of sites and pages, and not select others.

However, the blackout on information about search-engine crawl algorithms means we can only try to infer the character of these algorithms from search-engine selection patterns—an inexact exercise.

We have learned something of the nature of spider algorithms from a paper on efficient crawling by Cho, Garcia-Molina, and Page , presented at the WWW7 conference. This chapter, which discusses commonly used metrics for determining the "importance" of a Web page by crawling spiders, provides key insights relevant to the main claims of our chapter. Because of its significance, we discuss it here in some detail. Cho et al write:

Given a webpage P, we can define the importance of the page, I(P), in one of the following ways...:

1. *Similarity to a Driving Query Q*. A query Q drives the crawling process, and I(P) is defined to be the textual similarity between P and Q...
2. *Backlink Count*. The value of I(P) is the number of links to P that appear over the entire web. We use IB(P) to refer to this importance metric. Intuitively, a page P that is linked to by many pages is more important than one that is seldom referenced. On the web, IB(P) is useful for ranking query results, giving end-users pages that are more likely to be of general interest. Note that evaluating IB(P) requires counting backlinks over the entire web. A crawler may estimate this value with IB'(P), the number of links to P that have been seen so far.
3. *PageRank*. The IB(P) metric treats all links equally. Thus, a link from the Yahoo! home page counts the same as a link from some individual's home page. However, since the Yahoo! home page is more

important (it has a much higher IB count), it would make sense to value that link more highly. The PageRank backlink metric, IR(P), recursively defines the importance of a page to be the weighted sum of the backlinks to it. Such a metric has been found to be very useful in ranking results of user queries. We use IR′(P) for the estimated value of IR(P) when we have only a subset of pages available.

4. *Location Metric*. The IL(P) importance of page P is a function of its location, not of its contents. If URL u leads to P, then IL(P) is a function of u. For example, URLs ending with ".com" may be deemed more useful than URLs with other endings, or URL containing the string "home" may be more of interest than other URLs. Another location metric that is sometimes used considers URLs with fewer slashes more useful than those with more slashes. All these examples are local metrics since they can be evaluated simply by looking at the URLs."

The "*Similarity to a Driving Query Q*" metric uses a query term or string (Q)—such as "holiday cottages," for example—as the basic heuristic for crawling. This means that the spider does not need to make a decision about "importance" since it will be directed in its search by the query string itself. For our discussion, this metric is of minor significance. The real issue emerges when the crawling spider must "decide" importance without the use of a submitted query term. This is where the other metrics play the dominant role.

The *Backlink* metric uses the backlink (or inlink) count as its "importance" heuristic. The value of the backlink count is the number of links to the page that appear over the entire Web—for example the number of links over the entire Web that refers to http://

www.ibm.com. The assumption here is that "a page that is linked to by many [other] pages is more important than one that is seldom referenced."

Obviously, this is a very reasonable heuristic. We know from academic research that it is wise to look at the "canonical" works that is referred to—or cited in academic language—by many other authors. We know also, however, that not all topics necessarily have canons. Furthermore, although in some fields, a small number of citations may make a particular work a canon, in other fields, it takes a vast number of citations to reach canonical status. Thus, the *Backlink* heuristic would tend to crawl and gather the large topics/fields (such as 'shareware computer games') since an even relatively unimportant site in this big field will be seen as more "important"—have relatively more backlinks or inlinks—than an actually important site in a small field (such as "the local community services information"page) which would have relatively less backlinks or inlinks.

The essential point is that the large fields determine the measure, or threshold, of "importance"—through sheer volume of backlinks—in ways that would tend to push out the equally important small fields. (We will return to this issue, in our market discussion). With the *PageRank* metric this problem is exacerbated. Instead of treating all links equally, this heuristic gives prominence to back links from other 'important' pages—pages with high backlink counts. Thus, " since [a link from] the Yahoo! home page is more important (it has a much higher IB [backlink] count), it would make sense to value that link more highly."

In the analogy to academic papers, a metric like this would imply that a particular paper is even more important if referred to by others whom are already seen as important—by other canons. More simply, you are important if others who are already seen as important indicate that you are important. The problem with the *Backlink* and *PageRank* metrics is that they assume that backlinks are a reliable indication of importance or relevance. In those cases where authors of pages create links to other pages they see as valuable this assumption may be true.

There are, however, many organizations that actively cultivate backlinks by inducing Web-page creators to add a link to their page through incentives such as discounts on products, free software utilities, access to exclusive information, and so forth. Obviously not all Web-pages creators have equal access to the resources and incentive to induce others to link to them.

The *Location Metric* uses location information from the URL to determine "next steps" in the crawl. "For example, URLs ending with '.com' may be deemed more useful than URLs with other endings, or URL containing the string 'home' may be more of interest than other URLs."

Even though the authors do not indicate what they see as more important, one can assume that these decisions are made when crawl heuristics are set for a particular spider. It may therefore be of great significance "where you are located" as to how important you are seen to be. With the URL as the basis of decision making, many things can aid you in catching the attention of the crawling spider, such as having the right domain name, being located in the root directory, and so forth.

From this discussion on crawling metrics we can conclude that pages with many backlinks, especially backlinks from other pages with high backlink counts, which reside in locations seen as "useful" or "important" to the crawling spider, will become targets for harvesting.

Another criterion that seems to guide spiders is breadth or depth of representation. If a spider's algorithm favors breadth (rather than depth), it would visit more sites (or hosts) but index these only partially. In the case of big sites such as America On Line (AOL), Geocities, and so forth, spiders will index them at a rate of approximately 10-15%.

If your site is hosted on AOL or another big site there is a good chance that it will not be included. Another reason that a site, and so all the pages on that server, may be excluded from search engine databases is that the owner/Webmaster of that server has excluded robots through the robot exclusion standard by means of a "robots.txt" file.

This is often done because requests for pages from robots may significantly increase the load on a server and reduce the level of service to all other users. CNN, for example, excludes all robots from its site, as do many sites that offer free Web-page space. It is also important to note that harvesting robots of the search engines we looked at only process HTML files and in particular HTML tags.

Having said all of this it ought to be acknowledged that most spider based search engines do also allow autonomous submissions by Webmasters/designers. Software is available that automatically generates the required electronic formats and facilitates submission to a number of search engines simultaneously. This route has had very mixed results according to the Webmasters we spoke to.

On Being Ranked

Indexing is but one hurdle to clear for the creators of Web pages who strive for recognition through search engines. Having been successful in the indexing game, their concern shifts to ranking. Many observe that to be noticed by a person doing a search, a Web page needs to be ranked among the top 10-20 listed as hits. Because most search engines display the 10 most relevant hits on the first page of the search results, Web designers jealously covet those ten or twenty top slots. The importance of ranking is regularly discussed by leading authors in the field of web-site promotion:

> There is competition for those top ten seats. There is serious competition. People are trying to take away the top spots every day. They are always trying to fine tune and tweak their HTML code and learn the next little trick. The best players even know dirty ways to "bump off" their competition while protecting their own sites.

Although we have not found large-scale empirical studies measuring the effects of ranking on the behavior of seekers, we observe anecdotally that seekers are likely to look down a list and then cease looking when they find a "hit." A study of travel agents using computerized airline reservations systems, which showed an overwhelming likelihood that they would select a flight from the first screenful of search results, is suggestive of what we might expect among Web users at large.

Indeed if this were not the case it would be difficult to see why Webmasters are going to all the effort to get into the first screen; there is significant evidence that they do indeed take it very seriously. Now it may be that it is not only the first screen but could include the second and third screen as well. Nevertheless, even though we can not say without further research exactly where this line may be we can propose that it does matter whether you are in the first few screens rather than to much lower down the order. One could also argue such a position from an information overload point of view—we shall not pursue it here.

Relevancy ranking is an enormously difficult task. Some researchers working on search technologies argue that relevancy ranking is currently the greater challenge facing search engines and that developments in technical know-how and sheer capacity to find and index sites has not nearly been matched by the technical capacity to resolve relevancy ranking.

Besides the engineering challenges, experts must struggle with the challenge of approximating a complex human value ("relevancy") with a computer algorithm. In other words, according to these experts, while we seem to be mastering the coverage issue, we continue to struggle with the issue of what precisely to extract from the enormous bulk of possibilities for a given search.

Most ranking algorithms of search engines use both the position and the frequency of keywords as a basis for their ranking heuristics. Accordingly, a document with high frequency of keywords in the beginning of a document is seen as more relevant (relative to the keyword entered) than one with low frequency lower down in the document. Other ranking schemes, like the heuristic used by Lycos, are based on so-called "in-link" popularity.

The popularity score for a particular site is calculated on the total number of other sites that contain links to that site. High link popularity leads to an improved ranking. As with the crawl metrics discussed above one sees the standard or threshold of "relevance" being set by the big sites at the expense of equally relevant small sites.
The desire and battle for ranking have generated a field of knowledge called "search engine design," which teaches how to design a Web page in order to optimize its ranking and combines these teachings with software to assess its ranking potential.

On the one end of the spectrum, practices that make reasonable use of prima facie reasonable heuristics, help designers to optimize their Web pages' expected rankings when they are legitimately relevant to the person searching. On the other end of the spectrum some schemes allow Web designers to manipulate, or trick, the heuristics—schemes such as relevancy spamming, where Web-page designers "trick" the ranking algorithm into ranking their pages higher than they deserve to be ranked by means of keyword stuffing, invisible text, tiny text, and so forth. Such spamming activities doubly punish the innocent. If, for example, you design a Web page with a few graphic images at the beginning, followed somewhere toward the middle with text, you would be severely "punished" by the algorithm both because key terms are positioned relatively low down on the page and also because you would be competing for rank with those less, as it were, scrupulous in their designs.

Out of this strange ranking warfare has emerged an impossible situation: Search-engine operators are loath to give out details of their ranking algorithms for fear that spammers will use this knowledge to trick them. Yet, ethical Web-page designers can legitimately defend a need to know how to design for, or indicate relevancy to, the ranking algorithm so that those who search find what is genuinely relevant to their searches.

Beyond the challenge of second-guessing ranking algorithms, there may yet be another, more certain, method of getting results. Some producers of Web sites pursue other ways of elevating their ranking outside of the technical fray: They try to buy them. This subject is an especially sensitive one, and representatives of several major search engines indignantly deny that they sell search positions. Recently, however, in a much-publicized move, Alta Vista and Doublclick have invited advertisers to bid for position in their top slots.

Yahoo! sells prominence indirectly by allowing Web owners to pay for express indexing. This allows them to move ahead in the 6-month queue. Another method for buying prominence—less controversial but not unproblematic—allows Web owners to buy keywords for purposes of banner ads. Amazon Books, for example, has a comprehensive arrangement with Yahoo!, and Barnes & Noble with Lycos.

If a seeker submits a search to Yahoo! with the term "book" in it, or a term with a name that corresponds to an author's name, or book title in the Amazon database, he would get the Amazon banner (and URL) on his or her search result screen. This is also true for many other companies and products. The battle for ranking is fought not only between search engines and Web masters/ designers but also among organizations wishing for prominence.

There is sufficient evidence to suggest that the fierce competition for both presence and prominence in a listing has led to practices such as one organization retrieving a competitor's Web page, editing it so that it would not do well in the ranking, and resubmitting it as an updated submission, or one organization buying a competitor's name as a keyword and then having the first organization's banner and URL displayed when a search is done on that keyword.

Implications

We may wonder how all this affects the nature of Web users' experiences. Based on what we have learned so far about the way search engines work, we would predict that information seekers on the Web, whose experiences are mediated through search engines, are most likely to find popular, large, sites whose designers have enough technical savvy to succeed in the ranking game, and especially those sites whose proprietors are able to pay for various means of improving their site's positioning. Seekers are less likely to find less popular, smaller, sites, including those that are not supported by knowledgeable professionals.

When a search does yield these sites, they are likely to have lower prominence in rankings. These predictions are, of course, highly general and will vary considerably according to the keywords or phrases with which a seeker initiates a search, and this in turn, is likely to be affected by the seeker's competence with search engines. The nature of experiences of information seekers will also vary according to the search engines they choose. Some users may actively seek one search engine over others but some will simply, and perhaps unknowingly, use a default engine provided by institutions or Internet service providers (ISPs).

We are unlikely to find much relief from these robust regularities from meta search engines, like Metacrawler, Ask Jeeves, and Debriefing, because they base their results on existing search engines and normally accomplish their task by recognizing only higher order search keys than first-order engines. We note further that not only are most users unaware of these particular biases, they seem also to be unaware that they are unaware.

Readers may find little to trouble them in this description of search engine proclivities. What we have before us is an evolving marketplace in search engines: We ought to let producers of search engines do what they will and let users decide freely which they like best. Search engines whose offerings are skewed either because their selections are not comprehensive, or because they prioritize listings according to highest bid, will suffer in the marketplace. And even if they do not, the collective preferences of participants should not be second-guessed.

As the representatives of Yahoo! we cited earlier have argued, users' reactions must remain the benchmark of quality: Dissatisfied seekers will defect from an inadequate search engine to others that do a better job of indexing and prioritizing. Thus will the best search engines flourish; the poor ones will fade away from lack of use.

McChesney describes a comparable faith in the market mechanism as it applied to traditional broadcast media: "In the United States, the notion that commercial broadcasting is the superior system because it embodies market principles is closely attached to the notion that the market is the only 'democratic' regulatory mechanism, and that this democratic market is the essence of Americanism, patriotism, and all that is good and true in the world."

Both McChesney and Schiller, however, have criticized the idea that a media market best represents democratic ideals. In the case of search engines, we are, likewise, not optimistic about the promise of development shaped only by a marketplace. As anyone who has used search engines knows, the dominant search engines do not charge seekers for the search service.

Rather, the arrangement resembles that of commercial television where advertisers pay television stations for the promise of viewers. Similarly, search engines attract paid advertisements based on the promise of search usage. High usage, presumably, garners advertisers and high charges. To succeed, therefore, search engines must establish a reputation for satisfying seekers' desires and needs; this way they will attract seekers in the first place, and then will keep them coming back.

As a way of simplifying the discussion, however, we will refer to the marketplace as a marketplace in search engines with users, or seekers, as the buyers. This strategy does not, as far as we have been able to tell, alter the substantive outcomes of the particular issues we have chosen to highlight. We do not dispute the basic fact of the matter, namely, that a marketplace for search engines is possible.

It is also possible that such a market, reflecting discrepant degrees of satisfaction by seekers, will result in some search engines flourishing and others failing. Our dissatisfaction with this forecast is not that it cannot come true, but what it would mean, from the perspective of social values and the social investment in the Internet, if it did. Why, the critic might ask, on what grounds, would we presume to override the wishes of users so cleanly reflected in their market choices?

Our reply to this challenge, which we try to keep as free from sentimental prejudices as possible, cites two main sources of concern. One is that the conditions needed for a marketplace to function in a "democratic" and efficient way are simply not met in the case of search engines.

The other is our judgement that Web search mechanisms are too important to be shaped by the marketplace alone. We discuss each in turn, the first one only briefly. A virtue frequently claimed by defenders of the market mechanism is that participants are free to express their preferences through the choices they make among alternatives. Through their choices, incompetent inefficient suppliers are eliminated in favor of competent efficient suppliers.

As many critics have pointed out, however, this holds only for markets where those who supply goods or services have an equal possibility to enter the market and communicate with potential customers, and those who demand goods and services are fully informed and will act in a rational manner. Such an ideal market simply does not exist, and this is especially so in the case of search engines. If we focus on the demand side first, we see that most users of the Web lack critical information about alternatives. Only a small fraction of users understand how search engines work and by what means they yield their results.

It is misleading to suggest that these users are meaningfully expressing preferences or exercising free choice when they select from the alternatives. Though we lack systematic empirical evidence, the anecdotal results of asking people why they use or prefer one search engine to others is some version of, "It finds what I'm looking for," and a shrug.

Now if one is searching for a specific product or service it may be possible to know in advance how to determine that one has indeed found what one was looking for. When searching for information, however, it is difficult (if not impossible) to make such a conclusive assessment, since the locating of information also serves to inform one about that which one is looking for. This is an old information retrieval problem—often expressed as "how do you know what you do not know until you know it"—with which information science scholars have been battling for many years.

It seems unlikely that this would be different for search engines. In fact, the partiality of any search attempt will magnify this problem in the search-engine context. Not only this, we would also claim that users tend to be ignorant about the inherent partiality present in any search engine search results. They tend to treat search-engine results the way they treat library catalogue search results.

Given the vastness of the Web, the close guarding of algorithms, and the abstruseness of the technology to most users, it should come as no surprise that seekers are unfamiliar, even unaware, of the systematic mechanisms that drive search engines. Such awareness, we believe, would make a difference. Although here too we came across no systematic empirical findings, we note that in spheres outside of the electronic media, people draw clear and definitive distinctions between information and recommendations coming from disinterested, as compared with interested, sources, impartial advice as compared with advertisement.

Anecdotal experience bears this out as when customers learned that Amazon Books, for example, had been representing as "friendly" recommendations what were in reality paid advertisements. Customers responded with great ire and Amazon hastily retreated. The problem is equally complex on the supply side of the supposed market.

We have indicated the complex hurdles that need to be cleared to get listed and ranked appropriately. They all indicate that there simply is no level playing field by any stretch of the imagination. It seems clear that the "market will decide" view (problematic in most cases) is extremely problematic in this context. It is also doubtful weather this can be resolved to the point that the market argument will become valid.

The question of whether a marketplace in search engines approximates sufficiently a competitive free market is, perhaps, subordinate to the question whether we ought to leave the shaping of search mechanisms to the marketplace in the first place. We think this would be a bad idea.

Developments in Web searching are shaped by two distinct forces. One is the collective preferences of seekers. On the current, commercial model, search engines wishing to achieve greatest popularity would tend to cater to majority interests. While markets undoubtedly would force a degree of comprehensiveness and objectivity in listings, there is unlikely to be much market incentive to list sites of interest to small groups of individuals, such as individuals interested in rare animals or objects, individuals working in narrow and specialized fields, or, for that matter, individuals of lesser economic power, and so forth.

But popularity with seekers is not the only force at play. The other, is the force exerted by entities wishing to be found. Here, there is enormous inequality. Some enter the market already wielding vastly greater prowess and economic power than others. The rich and powerful clearly can influence the tendencies of search engines; their dollars can (and in a restricted way do already) play a decisive a role in what gets "found." For example, of the top 100 sites—based on traffic—just 6 are not ".com" commercial sites .

If we exclude universities, NASA and the U.S. government this drops to two. One could reasonably argue that the United Nations site ought to generate at least enough traffic to be in the list if we consider that Amazon is in position number 10 and USA Today in position 35.35 The cost to a search engine of losing a small number of searching customers may be outweighed by the benefits of pandering to "the masses" and to entities paying fees for the various forms of enhanced visibility.

We can expect, therefore, that at least some drift will be caused by those wishing to be found which, in turn, would further narrow the field of what is available to seekers of information, association, support, and services. It may be useful to think of the Web as a market of markets instead of as just one market. When we seek, we are not interested in "information" in general; rather we are interested in specific information related to our specific interests and needs.

Seekers might be in the market for information about, for example, "packaged tour holidays" or "computer hardware suppliers." For these markets, where we expect the demand for information to be great, we would expect the competition for recognition to be great as well.

Companies would pay high prices for the keyword banners that will ensure them the "top spot" and a search will generate many "hits" for the seekers. In contrast, there are other significantly smaller markets—for information about a rare medical condition, or about services of a local government authority or community. In this market of markets, there is likely to be little incentive to ensure inclusion for these small markets, and only a small cost (in loss of participation) for their exclusion.

Although we do not have empirical evidence, we would expect the law of Pareto to apply. We could imagine that a high percentage of search requests (say 80%, for argument's sake) are directed to a small percentage (say 20%) of the big markets, which would be abundantly represented in search results. Only a small percentage of the search requests (say 20%) might be addressed to the large percentage (say 80%) of the smaller markets, which would be underrepresented. This scenario would explain the limited incentive for inclusion and relatively low cost of exclusion. We find this result problematic.

A market enthusiast does not find this result problematic. This is exactly what the market is supposed to do; the range and nature of choices are supposed to ebb and flow in response to the ebb and flow of wants and needs of market participants—from varieties of salad dressings to makes of automobiles.

Nevertheless, we resist this conclusion not because we are suspicious of markets in general—for cars and salad dressings they are fine—but because maintaining the variety of options on the Web is of special importance. We resist the conclusion because we think that the value of comprehensive, thorough and wide-ranging access to the Web lies within the category of goods that Elizabeth Anderson describes in her book, *Values in Ethics and Economics* as goods that should not be left entirely (if at all) to the marketplace.

Anderson constructs an elaborate argument defending the claim that there are ethical limitations on the scope of market norms for a range of goods (and services). Abstracting principles from cases that are likely to be uncontroversial in this regard, for example, friendship, persons, and political goods (like the vote), she then argues that these principles apply to goods that are likely to be more controversial in this regard such as public spaces, artistic endeavor, addictive drugs, and reproductive capacities.

For some goods, such as cars, bottled salad dressings, etc., "unexamined wants," expressed through the marketplace, are a perfectly acceptable basis for distribution. For others, including those that Anderson identifies, market norms do not properly express the valuations of a liberal democratic society like ours, which is committed to "freedom, autonomy and welfare".

Although it is not essential to our position that we uncritically accept the whole of Anderson's analysis, we accept at least this: that there are certain goods—ones that Anderson calls "political goods," including among them schools and public places—that must be distributed not in accordance with market norms but "in accordance with public principles".

Sustaining the 80% of small markets that would be neglected by search engines shaped by market forces qualifies as a task worthy of public attention. Sustaining a full range of options here is not the same as sustaining a full range of options in bottled salad dressings, or cars, because the former enriches the democratic arena, may serve fundamental interests of many of the neediest members of our society, and more.

We make political decisions to "save" certain goods that might fall by the wayside in a purely market-driven society. In this way, we recognize and save national treasures, historic homes, public parks, schools, and so forth. In this spirit, we commit to serving groups of people, like the disabled, even though (and because) we know that a market mechanism would not cater to their needs.

We see an equivalent need in the case of search engines. In order to make the case convincing, however, we need to introduce into the picture a substantive claim because our argument against leaving search engines fully to the mercy of the marketplace is not based on formal grounds—or at least, we do not see them. We base our case against the "leave it to the market challenge" on the particular function that we see search engines serving and on the substantive vision of the Web that we think search engines ought to sustain. We do not argue unconditionally that the trajectory of search engine development is wrong or politically dangerous in itself, but rather that it undermines a particular, normative vision of the Web in society. Those who do not share in this vision are unlikely to be convinced that search engines are different from salad dressings and automobiles. The case that search engines are a special, political good presumes that the Web, too, is a special good.

Search engines, functioning in the manner outlined earlier, raise political concerns not simply because of the way they function, but because the way they function seems at odds with the compelling ideology of the Web as a public good. This ideology portrays the fundamental nature and ethos of the Web as a public good of a particular kind, a rich array of commercial activity, political activity, artistic activity, associations of all kinds, communications of all kinds, and a virtually endless supply of information. In this regard the Web was, and is still seen by many as a democratic medium that can circumvent the hegemony of the traditional media market, even government control.

Over the course of a decade, or so, computerized networks—the Internet and now the Web—have been envisioned as a great public good. Those who have held and promoted this vision over the course of, perhaps, a decade, have based their claims on a combination of what we had already achieved and what the future promises.

For example, with only a fraction of the population in the U.S. linked to the Internet, Al Gore promoted the vision of a Global Internet Infrastructure. This conception of the great public good—part-reality, part wishful thinking—has gripped people from a variety of sectors, including scholars, engineers and scientists, entrepreneurs and politicians. Each has highlighted a particular dimension of the Web's promise, some focusing on information, some on communication, some on commerce, and so on.

Although we cannot, here, enumerate all possible public benefits, we highlight a few. A theme that is woven throughout most versions of the promise is that the Web contributes to the public good by serving as a special kind of public space.

The Web earns its characterization as public in many of the same ways as other spaces earn theirs, and contributes to the public good for many of the same reasons. One feature that pushes something into the realm we call public is that it is not privately owned. The Web does seem to be public in this sense: its hardware and software infrastructure is not wholly owned by any person or institution, or, for that matter, by any single nation.

Arguably, it does not even come under the territorial jurisdiction of any existing sovereign state. There is no central or located clearinghouse that specifies or vets content, or regulates overall who has the right of access.

All those who accept the technical protocols, conform to technical standards (HTML, for example) and are able to connect to it may "enter" the Web. They may access others on the Web, and, unless they take special precautions, they may be accessed. When I post my Web pages, I may make them available to any of the millions potential browsers, even if, like a street vendor, I decide to charge a fee for entry to my page.

The collaborative nature of much of the activity on the Web leads to a sense of the Web not simply as unowned but as collectively owned. The Web fulfills some of the functions of other traditional public spaces—museums, parks, beaches, and schools. It serves as a medium for artistic expression, a space for recreation, a place for storing and exhibiting items of historical and cultural importance, and it can educate. Beyond these functions, the one that has earned it greatest approbation as both a public space and a political good is its capacity as a medium for intensive communication among and between individuals and groups in just about all the permutations that one can imagine, namely, one-to-one, one-to-many, etc.

It is the Hyde Park Corner of the electronic age, the public square where people may gather as a whole, or associate in smaller groups. They may talk and listen, they may plan and organize. They air viewpoints and deliberate over matters of public importance. Such spaces, where content is regulated by only a few fundamental rules, embody the ideals of the liberal democratic society.

The idea of the Web as a public space and a forum for political deliberation has fueled discussions on teledemocracy for some time. The notion of the public sphere as a forum in which communicatively rational dialogue can take place unsullied by ideology has had one of its strongest proponents in Habermas.

Although there is no universal agreement among scholars on the extent of effects the Web may have in the political sphere, several contributors to the debate have cited cases in which the Web appears to have had a decisive impact on the outcome. Douglas Kellner gives some examples: Zapatistas in their struggle against the Mexican government, the Tiananmen Square democracy movement, environmental activists who exposed McDonald's through the McLibel campaign, and the Clean Clothes Campaign supporting attempts of Filipino garment workers to expose exploitative working conditions.

We have not yet mentioned perhaps the dominant reason for conceiving of the Web as a public good, namely, its function as a conveyor of information. As a public means of access to vast amounts of information, the Web promises widespread benefits. In this so-called "information age," being among the information-rich is considered to be so important that some, like the philosopher Jeroen van den Hoven have argued that it makes sense to construe access to information as one of the Rawlsian "primary goods," compelling any just society to guarantee to a basic, or reasonable, degree of it to all citizens.

Growing use of the Web as a repository for all manner of information (e.g., government documents, consumer goods, scientific and artistic works, local public announcements, etc.) lends increasing weight to this prescription. The Web, according to the vision, is not intended as a vehicle for further expanding the gap between haves and have-nots, but for narrowing it.

The view of the Internet as a public good, as a globally inclusive, popular medium fueled much of the initial social and economic investment in the medium and its supporting technology, convincing progressive politicians to support it with investment and political backing. The vision has also motivated idealistic computer scientists and engineers to volunteer energy and expertise toward developing and promulgating the hardware and software, from the likes of Jonathan Postel, one the early builders of the Internet, who worked to keep its standards open and free, to professionals and researchers volunteering in efforts to wire schools and help build infrastructure in poorer nations. These inclusive values were very much in the minds of creators of the Web like Tim Berners-Lee:

> The universality of the Web includes the fact that the information space can represent anything from one's personal private jottings to a polished global publication. We as people can, with or without the Web, interact on all scales. By being involved on every level, we ourselves form the ties which weave the levels together into a sort of consistency, balancing the homogeneity and the heterogeneity, the harmony and the diversity. We can be involved on a personal, family, town, corporate, state, national, union, and international levels. Culture exists at all levels, and we should give it a weighted balanced respect at each level.

While the promise of the Web as a public space and a public good continues to galvanize general, political, and commercial support, many observers and scholars have cautioned that the goods are not guaranteed. The benefits of the vast electronic landscape, the billions of gigabytes of information, and the participation of millions of people around the world, depend on a number of contingencies.

Issuing one such caution, Lewis Branscomb calls for political effort to protect public interests against encroaching commercial interests. He worries about the enormous amount of money "invested in the new business combinations to exploit this consumer information market; the dollars completely swamp the modest investments being made in bringing public services to citizens and public institutions," urging federal, state and local government to "develop and realize the many non-profit public service applications necessary for the realization of the 'promise of NII'..

Gary Chapman and Marc Rotenberg, writing in 1993 on behalf of the organization Computer Professionals for Social Responsibility, listed a number of problems that would need to be solved before the National Information Infrastructure would be capable of serving the public interest. Of particular relevance to us here is Chapman and Rotenberg's reference to Marvin Sirbu's call for "Development of standardized methods for information finding:

White Pages directories, yellow Pages, information indexes." Without an effective means of finding what you need, the benefits of an information and communication infrastructure like the Web are significantly diminished. We can conjure up analogies: a library containing all the printed books and papers in the world without covers and without a catalogue; a global telephone network without a directory; a magnificent encyclopaedia, haphazardly organized and lacking a table of contents.

Search engines are not the only answer to this need but they still are the most prominent, the one to which most users turn when they want to explore new territory on the web. The power, therefore, that search engines wield in their capacity to highlight and emphasize certain

Web sites, while making others, essentially, disappear, is considerable. If search engines systematically highlight Web sites with popular appeal and mainstream commercial purpose, as well as Web sites backed by entrenched economic powers, they amplify these presences on the Web at the expense of others.

Many of the neglected venues and sources of information, suffering from lack of traffic, perhaps actually disappear, further narrowing the options to Web participants. If trends in the design and function of search engines leads to a narrowing of options on the Web—an actual narrowing or a narrowing in what can be located, the Web as a public good of the particular kind that many envisioned is undermined.

The ideal Web serves all people, not just some, not merely those in the mainstream. It is precisely the inclusivity and breadth that energized many to think that this technology would mean not just "business as usual" in the electronic realm, not merely a new tool for entrenched views and powers.

The ideal Web would extend the possibilities for association, would facilitate access to obscure sources of information, would give voice to many of the typically unheard, and would preserve intensive and broadly inclusive interactivity.

In considering the effects of a biased indexing and retrieval system, our attention first was drawn to the seekers. It is from the perspective of seekers that we noted the systematic narrowing of Web offerings: there would be fewer opportunities to locate various types of information, individuals and organizations, a narrowing of the full range of deliberative as well as recreational capabilities.

If access to the Web is understood as access by seekers to all of these resources, then the outcome of biased search engines amounts to a shrinking of access to the web. This perspective, however, does not represent all that is at stake. At stake is access to the Web in the shape of those, in addition, who would like to be found, to be seen and heard.

Marc Raboy describes this dimension of the new medium:

> The notion of "access" has traditionally meant different things in broadcasting and in telecommunications. In the broadcasting model, emphasis is placed on the active receiver, on free choice, and access refers to the entire range of products on offer. In the telecommunications model, emphasis is on the sender, on the capacity to get one's messages out, and access refers to the means of communication. In the new media environment, public policy will need to promote a new hybrid model of communication, which combines the social and cultural objectives of both broadcasting and telecommunications, and provides new mechanisms—drawn from both traditional models—aimed at maximizing equitable access to services and the means of communication for both senders and receivers.

The public good of the Web lies not merely in its functioning as a repository for seekers to find things, but as a forum for those with something to offer. The cost of a biased search-and-retrieval mechanism may even be greater for Web site owners wishing to be found—the senders.

Consider an example of just one type of case,

someone seeking information about, say, vacation rentals in the Fiji Islands. Because one rental is all he needs he is likely to look down a list of options and stop looking when he or she finds it. There is no loss to the seeker even if it turns out that lower down on the list there are many other candidates meeting his criteria. He has found what he or she needs. Those who are not found (because their lower ranking deprives them of attention or recognition) are offering, arguably, just as much value to the seeker. Our loss, in this case is twofold: One is that if continuing invisibility causes options to atrophy, the field of opportunity is thinned; the other is that many of those reaching out for attention or connection are not being served by web.

If search mechanisms systematically narrow the scope of what seekers may find and what sites may be found, they will diminish the overall value of the Web as a public forum, as well as a broadly inclusive source of information. Many have observed that to realize the vision of the Web as a democratizing technology, or, more generally, as a public good, we must take the question of access seriously.

Access is not merely a computer and a network hookup, as some have argued, nor in addition, the skills and know-how that enables effective use. Access implies a comprehensive mechanism for finding and being found. It is in this context that we raise the issue of the politics of search engines—a politics that at present seems to push the Web into a drift that does not resonate with one of the historically driving ideologies. We also believe we have shown why a rally to the market will not save the day, will not assure our grand purpose. The question of how to achieve it is far harder.

4

Computerization at Work

This chapter examines the extent to which computer-based systems are organized to enhance or degrade the quality of working life for clerks, administrative staff, professionals, and managers. Worklife merits alot of attention for four reasons.

First, work is a major component of many people's lives. Wage income is the primary way that most people between the ages of 22 and 65 obtain money for food, housing, clothing, transportation, etc. The United States' population is about 260,000,000, and well over 110,000,000 work for a living. So, major changes in the nature of work the number of jobs, the nature of jobs, career opportunities, job content, social relationships at work, working conditions of various kinds can affect a significant segment of society.

Second, in the United States, most wage earners work thirty to sixty hours per week — a large fraction of their waking lives. And people's experiences at work, whether good or bad, can shape other aspects of their lives as well. Work pressures or work pleasures can be carried home to families. Better jobs give people some room to grow when they seek more responsible, or complex positions, while stifled careers often breed boredom and resentment in comparably motivated people. Although people vary considerably in what kinds of experiences and opportunities they want from a job, few people would be thrilled with a monotonous and socially isolated job, even if it were to pay very well.

Third, computerization has touched more people more visibly in their work than in any other kind of setting — home, schools, churches, banking, and so on. Workplaces are good places to examine how the dreams and dilemmas of computerization really work out for large numbers of people under an immense variety of social and technical conditions.

Fourth, many aspects of the way that people work influence their relationships to computer systems, the practical forms of computerization, and their effects. For example, in our last section, Steven Hodas argued that the tenuousness of many teachers' classroom authority could discourage them from seeking computer-supported instruction in their classes. Also, Martin Baily and Paul Attewell argued that computerization has had less influence on the productivity of organizations because people integrate into their work so as to provide other benefits to them, such as producing more professional-looking documents and enhancing their esteem with others, or managers becoming counterproductive control-freaks with computerized reports.

When specialists discuss computerization and work, they often appeal to strong implicit images about the transformations of work in the last one hundred years, and the role that technologies have played in some of those changes. In nineteenth century North America, there was a major shift from farms to factories as the primary workplaces. Those shifts — often associated with the industrial revolution — continued well into the early twentieth century. Industrial technologies such as the steam engine played a key role in the rise of industrialism. But ways of organizing work also altered significantly. The assembly line with relatively high-volume, low-cost production and standardized, fragmented jobs was a critical advance in the history of industrialization. During the last 100 years, farms also were increasingly mechanized, with motorized tractors, harvesters and other powerful equipment replacing horse-drawn plows and hand-held tools. The farms also have been increasingly reorganized. Family farms run by small groups have been dying out, and have been bought up (or replaced by) huge corporate farms with battalions of managers, accountants, and hired hands.

Our twentieth century economy has been marked by the rise of human service jobs, in areas such as banking, insurance, travel, education, and health. And many of the earliest commercial computer systems were bought by large service organizations such as banks and insurance companies. During the last three decades, computer use has spread to virtually every kind of workplace, although large firms are still the dominant investors in computer-based systems. Since offices are the predominant site of computerization, it is helpful to focus on offices in examining the role that these systems play in altering work.

Today, the management of farms and factories is frequently supported with computer systems in their offices. Furthermore, approximately 50% of the staff of high tech manufacturing firms are white collar workers who make use of such systems — engineers, accountants, marketing specialists, etc. There is also some computerization in factory production lines through the introduction of numerically controlled machine tools and industrial robots. And certainly issues such as worklife quality and managerial control are just as real on the shop floor as in white collar areas. While the selections here examine white collar work, the reader can consider the parallels between the computerization of blue collar work and white collar work. Many of the studies of the computerization of blue collar work focus on factories. Factories employ a significant fraction of blue collar workers, but not a majority. Some of the major blue collar occupations that are not factory jobs include bus and truck drivers, heavy equipment operators, construction workers, appliance repair personnel, automobile and airplane mechanics, gas station attendants, dock workers, gardeners and janitors. Factories have been the site of some major computerization projects, as in the use of robots for welding and painting and the use of numerically controlled machinery. But many other blue collar jobs are being influenced by computerization as well.

The Transformation of Office Work

Office work has always involved keeping records. We don't have many detailed accounts of the earliest offices — that date back before the Middle Ages. Today, offices with dozens of clerks carrying out similar tasks are commonplace. Before the twentieth century, the majority of offices were small and were often the workplace of a single businessman or professional who kept informal records. The shape of offices the way work is organized, the role of women in their operation, the career lines, and office technologies has been radically transformed in the last 100 years.

Novelists like Charles Dickens have written some detailed descriptions of nineteenth century English clerks. They were often viewed as a dull bunch of sickly men who had safe but tedious jobs. In the nineteenth century, information was recorded by clerks using pen and ink, and copies were also made by hand. There were no powerful technologies for assisting one's hand in writing, copying, or even doing calculations. Filing systems were relatively makeshift, and there weren't standardized sizes of forms such as 3 x 5" cards or letter-size paper. Clerical work was a man's job, and was a common route for learning a business and becoming a potential owner.

In the early twentieth century, the technologies and organization of office work underwent substantial change. Firms began to adopt telephones and typewriters, both of which had been recently invented. By the 1930s and 1940s, many manufacturers devised electromechanical machines to help manipulate, sort and tally specialized paper records automatically. Some of the more expensive pieces of equipment, such as specialized card-accounting machines, were much more affordable and justifiable in organizations that centralized their key office activities.

While new equipment was often adopted to enhance the efficiency of offices, its use was tied to more widespread changes in the shape of organizations: the shifts in control to central administrators, and an increase in the number of jobs that were mostly being filled by women. Women began to work in offices as typewriter operators and clerks, and were typically viewed as short-term job-holders, working between school and marriage during their early to mid-twenties. As larger firms hired professional managers, many aspiring professionals turned to graduate schools rather than apprenticeships to learn their craft. Increasingly, specialized colleges rather than on-the-job training became the key entry point for professional and managerial careers. And with these careers dominated by males, clerical work became the province of women who could not readily move into the upper cadres of professional or managerial life.

This sketch indicates some of the key themes that permeate discussions of computerization and the quality of worklife: how efficient and flexible work will be, who controls the work that is done and how it is organized, how work is divided by gender, and who shares in the benefits of technological and organizational change.

Businesses such as insurance companies and banks, along with public agencies, adopted computer-based information systems on a large scale in the 1960s. Many of the early digital computer systems replaced electromechanical paper-card systems. The earliest systems were designed for batch operation. Clerks filled in paper forms with information about a firm's clients, and the forms were then periodically sent to a special group of keypunchers to translate the data onto cardboard cards. These "Hollerith cards" each stored one line of data, up to 80 characters. They were punched with a series of holes for each character or number. Keypunch machines were clanky devices with a typewriter-style keyboard, a bin for storing blank cards, and a holder for the card being punched. There was no simple way for a keypunch operator to correct an error. Cards containing errors (e.g., a letter "s" instead of an "a") had to be completely repunched. The punched cards were then taken to a data-processing department for a weekly or monthly "run", during which time records were updated and reports were produced. Errors often took a few cycles — sometimes weeks or months — to identify and correct. Using these early computerized systems required immense precision and care, since inaccuracies were detected and corrected very slowly. In addition, the data from one information system were usually formatted in a way that did not make them accessible to other systems. Professionals and managers often waited a few months for a new kind of report, and reports that required merging data from several separate systems were often viewed as prohibitively complex, time-consuming, and expensive to create. The earliest computer systems were speedier than the hand in processing large volumes of highly specialized transactions. But they were also very rigid and cumbersome for many people who used them.

Furthermore, the transaction-processing and report-generating programs were usually written by specialized programmers who were organized into specialized data-processing departments. Often, the large specialized computer systems, their operators, and their programmers were all located in basement offices — isolating them from organizational life. During the last 25 years, most organizations have reorganized their computer-based information systems to be more responsive and flexible, and to support a richer array of organizational activities. Terminals connected to shared data-bases or microcomput ers are commonplace in today's organizations.

During the 1980s and early 1990s, virtually every organization bought PCs and workstations. But "the PC revolution" did not just change the nature of office equipment it expanded the range of people who use computers routinely to include a much larger fraction of professionals (who are often men) — managers of all kinds, architects, accountants, lawyers, and so on. Many larger organizations are beginning to use computerized communication systems — like electronic mail — to help managers and professionals keep in contact when they are out of the office. And a few organizations are experimenting with pushing some of their staff out of regular offices and creating "virtual offices" in locations closer to their clients, their homes, and other more convenient (and less costly) locations.

In the last decade many larger organizations have been restructuring work. Some analysts tout these restructurings as byproducts of computerization. But many of these changes are often unrelated to computerization. For example, in the early 1990s many top managers have restructured their organizations so as to eliminate layers of managers below them ("delayering"). Some analysts argue that the use of electronic mail and computerized reporting systems has enabled this flattening of corporate hierarchies. Middle management in corporations that make relatively little use of electronic mail. If organizations can delayer without the use of e-mail, why would we believe that e-mail plays a key role in delayering?

Similarly, in the recent United States recession many organizations have laid off numerous workers, and the remaining staff often work much harder and much longer hours. It's not clear whether computerization has any significant influence on this pattern. Last, many organizations have restructured their employment contracts so that they have a much larger fraction of readily dispensable part-time and/or temporary employees than before the recent recession. This approach has created fewer full-time jobs with good career opportunities in specific organizations, and is probably unrelated to computerization.

Today, the typical clerk, professional or manager is much more likely to use a variety of powerful computer systems than would her counterpart ten and certainly fifteen years ago. But have jobs improved in a way that is commensurate with the technical improvement in computer systems? That is a key question which we will examine from several vantage points in this chapter.

Gender, Work and Information Technology

It may seem strange to begin a discussion of computerization and work with gender, when the common terms of computer use — such as "computer user" and interface — seem to be so gender neutral. But finding ways to talk about people's identities can help us understand computerization more deeply.

Discussions of women and computing often focus on clerical work because about one-third of the women in the work force are clerks. Conversely, about 80% of the 20 million clerks in the United States in 1993 were women. Women work in every occupation from janitors to ambassadors for the federal government, but they are not equally represented in the higher status and better paid professions. Less than 30% of the nation's 1.3 million programmers and systems analysts were women in 1993. But the nation's 16.1 million female clerks vastly outnumbered the nation's 412,000 female programmers and systems analysts in 1993. Female computer users today are more likely to be clerks who processes transactions, such as payroll, inventory, airline reservations, than to be information and computer professionals.

In the first selection, Suzanne Iacono examine how the dramatic improvements in office technologies over the past 100 years have sometimes made many clerical jobs much more interesting, flexible and skill-rich. But we also observe that these changes, especially those involving increased skill requirements, have not brought commensurate improvements in career opportunities, influence, or clerical salaries. We examine the actual changes in clerical work that have taken place over the last 100 years, from the introduction of the first typewriters through whole generations of office equipment — mechanical accounting machines, telephones, and photocopiers. Each generation of equipment has made certain tasks easier. At the same time, clerical work shifted from a predominantly male occupation, which provided an entry route to higher levels of management, to a predominantly female occupation that has been ghettoized. We criticize some of the technological utopians, such as Giuliano, by arguing that a new generation of integrated computer-based office systems will not automatically alter the pay, status, and careers of clerks without explicit attention. Further, we argue that computerization is a continuous processes which doesn't stop when a new kind of equipment is acquired.

These observations become more meaningful because the vast majority of working women are still concentrated in a few occupations, despite the growing numbers of women who have entered the professions and management in the last two decades. About 80% of the clerical workers in the United States in 1993 were women. In contrast, about 42% the executives and managers and 53% of the professionals were women. However, women professionals were clustered in nursing, social work, library jobs, and school teaching. For example, 75% of school teachers were women while less than 20% of architects were women. In 1988 only 30% of employed computer scientists and 10% of employed doctoral-level computer scientists were women and the percentages have not changed substantially since then.

The way that clerical work is computerized affects at 16 million working women in the United States . But men often believe that much of the work done in female work groups is trivial and can be readily automated. The problems in effectively computerizing such seemingly routine work that can, in fact, require managing subtle complexities of work processes actually effects a much larger number of people — both inside and outside the targeted work group.

Information Technology and New Ways of Organising Work

An important aspect of worklife is the issue of who controls the way that work is organized, the way that people communicate, and workers' levels of skills. In the 1980s, many professionals became enamored with microcomputers. They became the new electronic typewriter for writers of all kinds. Engineers set aside their slide rules and electronic calculators for software that mechanized their calculations and produced graphical data displays. Accountants helped drive the demand for microcomputers with their passion for computerized spreadsheets. And so on. Many professionals became hooked on the relative ease and speed of their computer tools, and dreaded any return to manual ways of working. They often adopted and adapted computers to their work in ways that enhanced their control over their work products. *Work still remained labor intensive,* since the working week did not diminish in length. Work sometimes became more fun, or at least less tedious.

In Giuliano's account, managers organized "industrial age" offices for efficiency, and will organize "information-age" offices in a way that enhances the quality of jobs as well. But some observers argue that managers will not give up substantial control to their subordinates. Andrew Clement, for example, argues that the close monitoring of employee behavior represents the logical extension of a dominant management paradigm — pursuit of control over all aspects of the business enterprise. Indeed some believe that to manage is to control. ". . . [M]anagement may be called 'the profession of control'".

Some authors argue that the industrialization of clerical work sets the stage for the industrialization of professional work as well. In "The Social Dimensions of Office Automation" Abbe Mowshowitz summarizes his sharp vision in these concise terms:

Our principal point is that the lessons of the factory are the guiding principles of office automation. In large offices, clerical work has already been transformed into factory-like production systems. The latest technology — office automation — is simply being used to consolidate and further a well-established trend. For most clerical workers, this spells an intensification of factory discipline. For many professionals and managers, it signals a gradual loss of autonomy, task fragmentation and closer supervision — courtesy of ccmputerized monitoring. Communication and interaction will increasingly be mediated by computer. Work will become more abstract . . . and opportunities for direct social interaction will diminish.

Some analysts have hoped that new computer communication technologies, such as electronic mail, would enable workers to bypass rigid bureaucratic procedures. Some analysts have found that electronic mail can give groups more ability to develop their own culture. And some have hoped that electronic mail would reduce the barriers to communication between people at different levels of hierarchy in an organization. But the evidence is mixed. Zuboff reports an interesting case that can dim these unbridled enthusiasms and lead us to ask under what conditions they are most likely to occur. In a large drug company she studied, managers claimed that their communications to electronic groups were often treated as policy statements, even when they wanted to make an informal observations or ad-hoc decisions. Further, when a group of about 130 professional women formed a private women's conference, male managers felt threatened, upper managers discouraged women from participating, and soon many participants dropped out.

That electronic communications systems are most likely to facilitate the formation of groups that upper managers deem to be safe, except in those special organizations — like universities and R&D labs — where there are strong norms against censorship. The controversy between technological utopians who see technologies as improving human and organizational behavior and those who see social systems as changing slowly in response to other kinds of social and economic forces will not be resolved by one or two case studies. But the cases are instructive to help focus the debate about what is possible and the conditions under which computer systems of specific kinds alter social life.

In "The Case of the Omniscient Organization," sociologist Gary Marx reports the behavior of a hypothetical company, Dominion-Swann (DS). The article, which is written as an excerpt from DS's 1995 Employee Handbook was originally published in the *Harvard Business Review*, a premier management magazine, in 1990 as the springboard for a discussion about information technology and management practices.

The DS case is constructed as a technologically anti-utopian narrative. But it also illustrates the power of well crafted utopian or anti-utopian narratives to highlight significant social choices. Marx crafted the DS case to illustrate how a business firm could develop a tight system of social control by partly relying upon relatively unobtrusive information technologies. However, the DS's 1995 Employee Handbook characterizes each form of control as either inoffensive or actually in employee's best interests.

In effect, DS has created an totally encompassing electronic prison in which virtually every aspects of an employee's behavior is continually monitored. Simultaneously, DS's 1995 Employee Handbook characterizes the company as a homelike community, where employees feel so comfortable with DS and each other, that continual monitoring of work practices, health, and social relations is simply a cozy part of everyday life. Marx has brilliantly portrayed the contradictions of some contemporary corporate cultures. DS would appear as hellish to an ardent individualist like William Whyte.

While Marx's portrait of DS can outrage and even terrify some people, it's not automatically true that a firm like DS would have trouble finding willing employees. North American society is very diverse, and many people live out social practices that would offend others in their own communities. And many firms have increased the extent to which they monitor some aspects of their employees work. Today, most of the monitoring focuses on measures of work, but some organizations also tap phone calls or eavesdrop on conversations between co-workers. A few organizations are even experimenting with "active badges" that would enable others to learn of their whereabouts at any time.

. The next selection "Mr. Edens Profits from Watching His Workers' Every Move" by Tony Horwitz describes a small financial services firm whose boss observes his employees by sitting behind their desks. Mr. Edens' techniques for having his employees work intensively by prohibiting them from looking at the window or conversing are very simple. But the fact that many people desperate for some kind of stable job will work for Mr. Edens suggests that employers that used techniques like Gary Marx's DS would also find willing employees.

In 1991, Grant and Higgens reported an empirical study about the effectiveness and repercussions of monitoring the activities of service workers, such as those who audit insurance claims. They studied a group of existing companies, none of which were as finely wired as the hypothetical DS. Grant and Higgens developed a rich, multidimensional concept of monitoring that includes features such as the granularity of data (i.e., amount of work per minute, hour, day or week) , the different types of data collected (i.e., work completed, error rates, customer complaints, nature of tasks), and the variety of people who routinely see data about a person's work (i.e., oneself, one's supervisor, one's peers, and/or upper managers). They found that many people did not object to computerized monitoring. And in a few cases, some people liked their work to be measured to help demonstrate how productive they actually were. But they also found that monitoring does not always improve performance and the quality of service. For example, extensive monitoring discouraged some people from being willing to help their co-workers with problems or work crunches. In fact, service seemed to degrade most when many aspects of performance were monitored and made available to supervisors. Grant and Higgens view monitoring as a legitimate but subtle form of managerial intervention that can often backfire when system designers and managers do not pay close attention to people's indirect responses to monitoring.

Control Over the Location of Work

It is possible for managers to work with several competing logics. They may be concerned with maintaining some control over their subordinates time and pay, but also with allowing sufficient flexibility and self-direction to insure good quality work and retain good employees. In fact, some organizations try to pay less by offering attractive working conditions. One of the interesting possibilities of computerized work work at home seems to have gotten stalled because of dilemmas of workplace control. Many self employed people work at home. Futurists like Alvin Toffler have been specially excited by the possibilities that people who normally commute to a collective office could elect to work at home. In *The Third Wave,* Toffler portrayed homes with computer and communications equipment for work as "electronic cottages".

A recent report developed under the auspices of the Clinton administration included a key section, "Promoting Telecommuting," that lists numerous advantages for telecommuting (IITF, 1994). These include major improvements in air quality from reduced travel; increased organizational productivity when people can be more alert during working hours faster commercial transit times when few cars are on the roads; and improvements in quality or worklife. The benefits identified in this report seem so overwhelming that it may appear remarkable that most organizations have not already allowed all of their workers the options to work at home.

Forester critiqued the visions of full-time work at home via telecommuting as a romantic preference. After coming to appreciate the social isolation reported by several people who worked at home full time, he speculates that many analysts who most enthusiastically champion full time work at home with computing have never done it themselves. There have been several published studies of the pros and cons of firms giving their employees computer equipment to use at home while communicating with their shared offices via electronic mail. Some analysts hoped that work at home will decrease urban congestion during computer hours, give parents more opportunity for contact with young children, and allow people to spend more time in their neighborhoods. However, people who work a substantial fraction of the time at home may be unavailable for meetings, may be less visible to their peers and (therefore) passed over for promotions, and may be difficult to supervise unless they work on a piece-rate system. And some employees may lack sufficient self-discipline for work at home.

Many popular accounts focus on the way that home can be a less distracting place to work than the collective office. Homes are different kinds of places to work than offices. Homeworkers report a different set of attractions and distractions at home: sociable neighbors may expect to be able to drop in any time; the refrigerator may beckon others too frequently; a spouse who works in an office may expect the partner at home to cook dinner nightly, the child who comes home from school at 3PM may want immediate attention, and so on. Some parents choose to work at home because they can spend time with their babies and pre-school children, but they often get much less done than at their collective offices. Olson's study of full time work at home by computer professionals exemplifies some of the empirical studies. She found reduced job satisfaction, reduced organizational commitment and higher role conflict in her sample. She also wonders whether work-at-home practices can exacerbate workaholism.

A few firms, such as IBM and Chiat/Day, have conducted pilot tests of the telecommuting and "virtual offices". And the members of a few occupations, such as journalists, professors, salesmen, and accountants often take notebook computers on the road when they travel. But the vast majority of firms keep their office-bound work force keystroking in the office rather than at home. Some workers are given computer equipment to use for unpaid overtime work. To date, however, no large firms have dispersed a large fraction of their full-time work force to their homes to work with computer systems.

It seems that the desire to maintain control underlies many managers' fears of having their employees work full-time at home. It is much easier for managers to be sure that their subordinates are putting in a fair day's work in an office from nine to five (sometimes called "face work"), than to develop and monitor subtle contracts about the amount of work ("deliverables") to be produced each week or month.

Anthropologist Connie Perin adds an interesting insight about the complexities of off-site work after interviewing about 150 managers and professional employees in a variety of occupations, all organizationally employed, full-time workers in several United States industries. She found that

> Field-based employees typically complain of their "isolation" from a central office which "never understands" the conditions of their work— that lack of empathy or interest represents a fundamental negativism toward office absence. Those not working in a central office may be regarded as quasi-employees, similar to contract, part-time, or temporary employees within the organization .... Overall, both physical and social distance, independent of all other considerations, attenuates organizational legitimization and managerial trust.

Electronic mail seems to give greater visibility to people who work at home. But the technology only facilitates communication, and effective communication requires additional skills and attention. And there may be some subtle gender biases in electronic discussion groups. Some telecommuters have gone as far as making videos of their homes to show their supervisors their working conditions.

In addition, some people find social and technological attractions to working in a group office. A shared office is often populated with people to chat or go to lunch with, especially when it is compared with the typical isolating suburban neighborhood where many telecommuters live. In addition, organizations usually provide better computer equipment, including higher-speed computer networks and faster laser printers in shared offices than in their employees' homes. Last, today's computer equipment is still relatively clumsy and occasionally unreliable. It is much easier to get meaningful help from a colleague who can see one's work, or even from a technical support person at the office, than by explaining subtle problems over a telephone. Any of these patterns could be altered, but they each require changing many conventions of organizational and neighborhood organization.

"Promoting Telecommuting" is infused with a decent enthusiasm for "doing the right thing," but fails to come to terms with many of the significant institutional issues that inhibit significant telecommuting. Conceptually, it relies upon rational systems models of organizations rather than the natural systems models of organizations. The report encourages Federal agencies to take the lead in creating telecommuting programs with their employees, especially in large metro areas with substantial air pollution. And it will be interesting to see whether these pilot projects scale up to include a significant work force and if they are sustainable.

It is still an open question whether many organizations will allow substantial fractions of their work force to work at home with computing part time (one to three days a week), for reasons of personal flexibility or to facilitate regional transportation plans.

Few homes are designed for significant home offices, and there are many important questions about the pros and cons of part time work-at-home with computing (and fax) for those who prefer this option.

New Forms of Work Organisation

This section began with the controversies about the ways that computerization changes the organization of work. This debate used traditional forms of regimented assembly lines as a major reference point. Another related controversy is the extent to which new computing technologies, especially those that support communications open up new forms of work. Does electronic mail eliminate organizational hierarchies and facilitate the formation of flexible (virtual) work groups? Do new forms of computerization create novel possibilities for organizational learning?

There are few empirical studies that support these speculations, and the existing evidence is mixed. In one intriguing study, Tom Finholt and Lee Sproull found that electronic mail can give groups more ability to develop their own culture. Others argue that electronic mail reduces the barriers to communication between people at different levels of hierarchy in an organization.

The controversy about the possibility of computerization fostering new forms of work organization is very engaging. Enthusiasts of the position that computerization can lead to new forms of work have the advantage of offering exciting possibilities. However, they rarely face the issues of workplace and support systems for technical work. When they ignore recurrent themes from previous eras of computerization, they risk being blindsided by perennial issues in new guises.

The Design and Routine Use of Computerized Technologies

There are relatively few published studies of the ways that people actually use software systems in their work — which features do they use, to what extent do they encounter problems with systems or gaps in their own skills, how do they resolve problems when difficulties arise, how does the use of computerized systems alter the coherence and complexity of work?

There does not seem to be single simple answers to these questions. Some organizations computerize some jobs so as to make them as simple as possible. An extreme example is the way that fast food chains have computerized cash registers with special buttons for menu items like cheeseburgers and malts so that they can hire clerks with little math skill. Kraut, Dumais, and Koch report a case study of customer service representatives in which simplifying work was a major consequence of computerization.

But it is common for images of simplification to dominate talk about computerization, regardless of the complexity of systems. Clement reports a case of computerization for secretaries in which managers characterized new systems as "super typewriters" which didn't require special training; they were very mistaken. Many of the popular "full featured" PC software packages for text processing, spreadsheets, and databases include hundreds of features. Narratives which focus on the capabilities of systems usually suggest that people can readily have all the advantages that all the features offer; actual behavior often differs from these expectations. Most people who use these powerful programs seem to learn only a small fraction of the available capabilities — enough to do their most immediate work. Moreover, it is increasingly common for many workers to use multiple computer systems, often with conflicting conventions, further complicating people's ability to "use computer systems to their fullest advantage." Some of these dilemmas can be resolved when organizations adopt relatively uncomplicated systems, train their staffs to use them, and provide consulting for people who have questions. However, many managers believe that supporting computer use with training and consulting is too expensive. Training is not cheap; an organization may pay $500 in labor time for a professional to learn to use a package that costs $150 to purchase.

For example: a research administrator of a major food processing firm who was using a popular and powerful spreadsheet to budget projects. He wanted to print out reports in different fonts, such as printing budget categories in larger bolder print. But he was puzzled how to do this. He knew that "it could be done" because he saw such a report in an advertisement. He treated his ignorance as a personal failing. He would have had to learn his spreadsheet's macro facility to produce this effect, and there was no clue in his manual about the appropriate strategy. In some organizations he might have turned to an information center with skilled consultants. But in his organization, the PC consultants were already overworked just installing new PCs and had no time to train users or consult on software use. This was not a critical problem for the manager. But it is indicative of the way that many organizations expect white collar workers to learn to effectively use computer systems on their own, with little support besides limited manuals and advice from co-workers. Most computer systems do not work perfectly, further complicating what users have to learn and how they integrate systems into their work.

The selection by Poltrock and Grudin goes behind the scenes of a major software development firm to examine the way that software is designed and built in practice. They describe published principles of software development, such of those of John Gould, that emphasize close contact with the people who will actually use a software package (or surrogates) at all stages of design and testing. But they observe an odd contradiction in the practical work of many software developers. Many software developers claim that these principles are obvious, but they rarely follow them in practice. Poltrock and Grudin's study examines how such a contradiction can happen in practice. It could be that software developers behave like those of us who know that we should always balance our checkbooks, but often let it slip when we're busy. Their case study examines how computer scientists who were designing CAD software work within a structured organization. They are not autonomous masters of their own designs. People in other departments also play key roles in shaping the resulting product. In this case, the marketing department was able to seize the role as the group that would speak for people who would use the CAD system. They quote one software engineer, who noted:

> "I think it would be worthwhile if all developers would spend maybe a couple of hours a year seeing how the product is used by those customers. Just watching them. And while they're watching them the customer would say, 'I don't like the way this works,' and noting those things.... You need to see how they use it. You need to understand, first of all,

> what they're doing. So you need them to give you a little background, and then watch how they accomplish it, and see the totality of it, especially. How they fire up, the whole structure of their day. And then use that information to give you a global sense of how to help them out. You can't help them without understanding how they work."

This comment poignantly portrays the isolation of many software designers for whom spending just "a couple of hours a year" with their customers would be a major improvement in their abilities to develop higher quality software.

In the next selection, MIS Professor Christine Bullen and John Bennett (then employed by IBM) follow this advice. They examine the ways that people actually integrate computer systems to support collaborative work in groups (groupware) into their work. They report how several work groups have attempted to use some of today's best commercially available groupware systems with mixed results. Their informants often report that they value the electronic mail features of these systems as most important, even though each of these systems has many other advertised features. But many groups have found other features hard to use routinely, or simply not worth the effort.

More significantly, Bullen and Bennett report that many groups slowly learned that they would have to reorganize their work in order to take best advantage of their groupware. For example, the usage of electronic calendars to schedule meetings requires that all participants keep detailed calendars up to date on the computer system, even if they often spend much of their days out of the office. Many managers and professionals hope that they can computerize effectively by installing appropriate equipment, rather than by reorganizing work when they (re)computerize. Bullen and Bennett make a provocative attempt to characterize those groups which are high performers: they are not always the most computerized. They argue that group members and their managers have worked hard to create work environments which have "clear elevating goals," and which support and reward commitment. These groups have developed effective social systems with coherent goals and related rewards as well as adopting technologies which might help improve their performance.

There is considerable unpublished controversy about this kind of analysis, since many technologists and computer vendors try to convince computer using organizations that appropriate new technologies alone will improve working styles and organizational effectiveness. During the 1990s interesting technologies such as expert systems, groupware and graphical interfaces will be written about by technologists and journalists as if they can significantly improve the ways that people work without requiring important changes in the way that groups organize their work. Careful studies of work with new computing technologies, like Bullen and Bennett's study, suggests that new technologies alone are unlikely to be magic potions which can automatically improve work just by appearing in a workplace.

Social Design of Computerized Systems and Work Settings

An exciting recent development is the effort by some researchers and practitioners to conceptualize the design of computer and networked systems as a set of interrelated decisions about technology and the organization of work. Managers and professionals who focus on the use of computing may find that this approach fits their routine practices. But thinking and talking about computerization as the development of socio-technical configurations rather than as simply installing and using a new technology is not commonplace.

Many professionals use computer technologies which expand the range of their work methods. The adoption of electronic mail to facilitate communication between people who work in different time zones and the acquisition of compact portable computers to facilitate working on the road are two routine illustrations. But organizations that adopt portable computers and e-mail to improve the flexibility of people's work relationships must do more than simply acquire technologies to realize these specific advantages. For example, portable computers may help people work outside of their offices. Some of the resulting convenience hinges on technological choices, such as acquiring machines which run software whose files are compatible with file formats used in the office. But much of the resulting flexibility depends upon social choices as well. For example, if organization A requires men and women to report to work daily during regular working hours even when they have the portable computers, then people gain relatively little flexibility in work location if that policy is not also changed. People may be able to take portable computers home after hours or on weekends, or on the road while they travel. Thus, organization A may gain some unpaid overtime work with these policies. But the men and women who work in organization A will not gain much of the "control over the location of work" which people many attribute to portable computing. In contrast, if organization B allows its employees to work at places and times which they choose, then its employees can use portable computing to have even more flexibility in their work.

In each of these cases, the men and women who adopt the equipment and construct work policies and practices for organizations A and B have created distinct socio-technical configurations — or social designs. And these social designs which incorporate portable computing, rather than the technology alone, have different consequences.

Analytical research about computerization in organizations, as well as our own systematic observations, has helped identify many arenas in which organizational participants make *social choices* about the socio-technical configurations of their computerized and networked systems. The term "social design of computerized systems," or "social design," characterizes the joint design of both the technological characteristics of a computerized systems and the social arrangements under which it will be used.

The social design of work systems with computing does not necessarily improve the quality of peoples' work lives. For example, some managers have computerized relatively routinized clerical work by fragmenting jobs and tightening supervisors' abilities to monitor the quality, pace and speed of people's work. These same managers may develop good systematic training programs for the clerks whose work is now more regimented. However, social design can also be very benign. It encourages participants in a computerization project to review the web of practices and policies related to computing which can otherwise be "unanticipated."

Two of the major approaches to social design contrast strongly in their assumptions about people, organizations, technology and work. *Business Process Reengineering* is usually applied by managers and consultants to streamline operations. The main aims of these reengineering projects seem to be reducing the time for a specific business process, such as dispatching a repairman to a site or processing an insurance claim, and also reducing the number of people who work on that activity. However, some consultants have promised more diverse financial benefits to their clients (and potential clients).

David Schnitt characterizes a business process in these terms:

> A business process is best defined as an activity in the organization fundamental to operating the business that serves an internal or external customer and has a well-defined outcome or series of outcomes. Every organization is made up of business processes. Examples include such mundane activities as accounts payable, inventory control, field service, or the processing of a customer application .... Since many work steps in business processes are executed by people in different departments; this view encourages a cross-functional perspective....the business process view of the Accounts Payable (A/P) process sheds new light on it as a complicated, slow, error-prone process involving many different departments and personnel. It reveals that the process is really the procurement process, not just A/P. Seen from this perspective, the opportunities

> for improvement are much greater. The key is to focus on the value-added outcome of the process (why it is done, not what is done) and how it relates to other processes in the organization.

Business process reengineering brings an industrial engineering perspective to the design of organizations and work. The flow of documents and authorizations are key elements, and the character of people's jobs is a secondary consideration in much of the writing about this approach to redesigning organizations. Computer systems of various kinds are often key elements of a reengineering project, including scanners and document processing systems at the "front end" of a process, and the use of workflow software to model and mange some of the subsequent activity.

The analyses which support these projects usually rest on Rational systems models of organizations to examine workflows that run across departments. They usually examine few influences on worklife and work organization other than those that directly pertain to reliable and efficient workflows.

The major alternative approach, sometimes called socio-technical systems design, makes people and their relationships in support of work, rather than workflows, the center of organizational reforms with information technology. Peter Keen articulates this approach in these terms:

> The business team, rather than the functionally defined hierarchy or the dotted-line or matrix-management variants that show up on the organization chart, is increasingly being seen as the real unit of organizing. Business is finally recognizing that division of labor is increasingly

> ineffective as the basis for an organization in an environment of constant rather than occasional change and of shifting functions to the proven project and team-based processes long employed by the research and technical functions. Teamwork is relational; the quality of performance rests on the quality of interactions, communication, and coordination among team members....

Instead of focusing on organization structure, business today needs to look at the mechanisms that make communication simple, flexible...IT makes practical many of the visions of management thinkers. The management principles for exploiting IT organizational advantage require a basic rethinking of old assumptions—especially concerning the links between strategy and structure—at the top of the firm.

Flexibility and adaptability are the new watchwords for organizations and for people. Firms that do not attend to their people's careers as well as their jobs might well have to replace much of their work force. Their human capital will be a depreciated resource, one they may find harder to replenish than they thought.

Keen's analysis appeals to many professionals. One technologically oriented corollary leads some computer scientists to develop designs for computer systems which facilitate communication and collaboration in diverse forms: mail systems, conferencing systems, co-authoring systems, and so on. But it is much too facile to think that lower status workers, such as clerks and semi-professionals are most appropriately targeted with business process reengineering while only higher status workers, such as managers and professionals, can bask in a more supportive and enriched relational organization.

For example, Jim Euchner and Patricia Sachs recently reported the redesign of a "work system" in which a regional United States phone company (NYNEX) provided customers with high speed (T.1) phone service. The installation required the collaboration of over 40 people in five distinct departments. NYNEX took much longer to complete these installations than their competitors, and rapidly lost significant market share in New York City. A computerized scheduling system had been used to assign different technicians to their specialized activities in the installation and fine-tuning of the T.1 lines in customers' offices. A large part of the delay seemed to derive from the way that some key problems cut across the domains of different technicians — they were either problems at system interfaces, or problems whose causes were somewhat ambiguous. The computer system helped to efficiently schedule the technicians' trips to the site — one at a time — to give them full and balanced workloads. It did not help bring together the specific technicians who would be needed to solve the more vexing installation problems.

A group from NYNEX's Science and Technology Center collaborated in a socio-technical design with both the craft workers and managers who were responsible for T.1 installations to develop a new "work system design." Some of the principles of work system design that they articulated are common themes in many socio-technical systems projects. For example, they had craft workers who do the actual work, as well as more senior managers, design the new work system and implement it. They focussed on workflows and whole processes rather than upon discrete tasks, a concept which is shared with many business process reengineering projects. However, they sought to provide people with ownership and responsibility for whole jobs, rather than discrete tasks. And they developed some specific guidelines for designing computer and communication systems: to support workflows and communications; to provide "intelligent" information handling; and to have interfaces that match the language in which people conceptualize their work.

The new T.1 work system reorganized the installations around cross-functional teams who have joint responsibility for insuring that installations are prompt and effective. The team's composition is rather fluid and can depend upon the specific customer and the stage of the installation. But they usually mix both white collar and blue collar workers, and can include people at different managerial levels. The coordination relies upon people scheduling technicians rather than upon computerized scheduling, although computer support is provided for other activities. In this particular case, the work system was redesigned, while the existing computer systems were left untouched.

Jewett and Kling report the case of a pharmaceutical firm in which sales managers radically restructured the responsibilities of sales clerks from passive order-takers to be more proactive sales representatives. The department held extensive meetings to reconceptualize their roles, and the staff rewrote all of the job descriptions.

The resulting jobs were enriched and also reclassified at somewhat higher pay levels. The department's managers also commissioned the development of a new computerized information system to provide richer searching capabilities to support the restructured jobs. In this case, the configuration of the information systems was part of a larger social design which included the explicit reconceptualization of key jobs.

These socio-technical strategies require that systems analysts and designers understand many of the work practices, schedules, resource constraints, and other contingencies of the people who will use the new computerized systems. Some organizations, such as NYNEX, have included social scientists on their design teams to facilitate such observation and understanding. They also recommend that people who use the systems have a substantial role in specifying their designs as well as altered work practices.

One reason that stand-alone microcomputers may have been so attractive for many people is that they offered more control over the form of computerization and changes in work than systems which ran on shared computer systems. In addition, microcomputer users' work methods made them less dependent upon having access to busy full time computer professionals to design and modify systems. This made their computing arrangements more adaptable. Many organizations implemented PC systems with a tacit social design that gave their workers more autonomy.

The next two selections by anthropologist Lucy Suchman and computer scientist Andrew Clement give us some deeper insights into socio-technical work design. In "Supporting Articulation Work." Lucy Suchman examines the way that critical work processes are often invisible to casual observers. In a telling examples that appears in the middle of her article, Suchman contrasts the way that lawyers and legal assistants in a firm view the work of coding legal documents with "objective categories" such as From, To, and Date. The male lawyer viewed the coding task as mindless, work that could be done "by chimpanzees" or "by 9-year olds." The lawyer viewed legal interpretation as mindful work. In contrast, the female legal assistants showed Suchman that the tasks of identifying which set of papers should be considered as a document, which names on the papers should be labelled as To and From, and which date should serve as the documents' official date all required mindful interpretation. Suchman notes that it is common for male workers to create artificial categories, such as mindful/mindless or hard/easy to create status boundaries. She goes on to describe how she and her research team developed a prototype document imaging system whose key features were based on the document coding task as experienced by the coders.

In "Computing at Work: Empowering Action by 'Low-level Users'" Andrew Clement describes how several different groups of clerks participated in the design of computer systems in their work. The opportunity to participate was not generously initiated by upper managers in any of these cases. In the case of the Manitoba (Canada) Telephone System (MTS), managers developed a "pervasive command and control culture in which (mostly female) operators were ... constantly watched over and punished for every infraction of the rules." In 1986, operators began reporting health problems, and even stopped work in one office after they became frightened of unsafe working conditions. A Canadian health authority and the clerk's union helped negotiate the opportunity for redesigning work in a Trial Office" with upper managers. Clement reports the resulting change that "operator services have been reorganized around smaller, multi- function work groups while several of the innovations first adopted by the Trial Office — e.g. elimination of remote monitoring, improved training resources, cross training, unlimited rights to trading shifts, greater discretion in responding to customer queries — are being extended throughout MTS."

Clement describes two other projects in a library systems and in a university administration which clerks were able to convince upper managers to allow them to redesign their worn work and computer support systems. He notes some important commonalities in these cases:

For all the differences between these three cases in terms of the jobs, technologies and organizational setting, there are striking similarities. In each, women office workers faced unnecessary hardships because of conventional ways in which computerization had been imposed on them. They had not been consulted about the introduction of the computer systems in the first place, and initially tried to accommodate to the new conditions, in spite of experiencing considerable adverse effects - effects that are commonly associated with the negative implications of computerization elsewhere.

Coming from the lower reaches of rigid, strongly hierarchical organizations, attempts to voice concerns were met with fates typical of bottom-up initiatives. It was only after pressures for change had grown considerably was any action taken.

The high side of these "participatory design" projects was that the clerks in each of these organizations were able to create more productive and less regimented jobs for themselves. These kinds of working conditions are sometimes taken for granted by higher status professionals.

In a more recent paper, Andrew Clement and Pater Van den Besselaar examined the results of many participatory work-redesign design projects. In many cases specific projects lead to participants improving their understanding of information technologies and effectively proposing new or altered systems that improved their working conditions. However, many of these projects were relatively short term, and most of them were isolated examples within their larger organizations. Participatory design is a fundamentally controversial approach because its advocates forthrightly question traditional lines of authority and typical assumptions about who has expertise in organizations.

A third approach to social design is congruent with both business process reengineering and socio-technical design: web analyses of computing infrastructure. One key insight of this approach is that social designs which focus primarily on the overt work system, such as processing an insurance claim or installing a phone line, can overlook the kinds of systems and support which are critical for making computer and communications systems workable for people.

For example, in a study of computing and organizational practices in a large number of leading companies, McKersie and Walton observe, "Despite widespread recognition among IT planners that most systems are underutilized because of inadequate training, the deficiency is repeated in systems implementation after systems implementation." Training is only one element of infrastructure for computing support. Web analysis locates computer systems and people who use them in a matrix relationships with other people, organizations and technologies on which they depend.

Computing infrastructure can play a key role in social designs. A group may prefer a high performance computing application which requires substantial training and consulting, or a medium performance application which people may learn more effectively on their own. Whichever application is chosen makes subsequent demands upon computing infrastructure for those work groups. Organizations often fail to realize the gains from IT that they hope for when they: a) select high performance applications and fail to provide needed support or training in their use; or b) select lower performance applications but still do not encourage people to experiment and learn in their workplaces. My case study of computerization in a research team illustrates how a Natural systems model of organizations is needed to understand what kinds of infrastructure are feasible for specific work groups and work systems. This case was specially complex because the work groups' computing facilities, including PCs, printers, and e-mail systems, were administered by several different organizations and located in dispersed locations.

Computing practices can be very complex in practice. It is one thing to say that you computer network has a high speed printer, and another thing to use it effectively when it is located 1/2 mile away or in an office which is often locked when you work. The remarkable examples in which people who worked in hi-tech organizations forwarded e-mail and files via the Internet to their spouses who worked 20 miles away so they could get printed copies within a day. Printing messages and files that they received over their networks proved to be elusive in their own organizations! It is easiest for us to imagine that someone who uses e-mail can routinely attach files, print messages, file copies of inbound and outbound messages in special folders, send messages to groups, and so on. It is remarkable how many e-mail systems are configured in ways that make these seemingly routine activities cumbersome or virtually impossible for many men and women who use them.

The analysts who facilitate social designs use tacit models of organizational behavior. Business process reengineering often rests upon Rational Systems models. Since one overt goal of many of these projects is reducing the number of people employed in an area (often referred to as "downsizing" or "decapitation"), it should not be very surprising that the people who will do redesigned work are often unenthusiastic about sharing their best insights with designers.

Natural Systems models of organizations take much more explicit account of people's social behavior (such as seeking occupational security, careers, and specific kinds of economic and social rewards from work). Natural systems models also underlie many of the socio-technical design projects.

During the next decade organizations will continue to computerize work — automating new activities and replacing earlier systems with newer technologies. The controversies about how to change work with computer systems will continue to have immense practical repercussions. This chapter identified some of the key controversies that pervade this diffuse literature — those that pertain to gender equity, control, support systems, social design and new ways of organizing work. Many of the controversies are implicit, since authors often take positions without carefully discussing the alternative positions and debates.

Further systematic research can help resolve some controversies, such as the possibilities of effective social design, the conditions which engender new forms of work organization, and the extent to which they create higher quality workplaces. However, these controversies also pertain to the concrete behavior of organizations, and questions about what they do and will do, not just what they should do.

Organizations and workplaces differ and consequently, their appropriate work organization technologies differ. The research shows that no single logic has been applied towards changing work with computerization. So key controversies cannot be automatically resolved by a new kind of computer technology, such as pen-based systems, or voice recognition. New technologies create new opportunities, but do not always require that the opportunities will be exploited, for better or worse. For example, the research shows that few organizations utilize fine grained computer monitoring systems as intensively as critics of automated monitoring suggest. On the other hand, relatively few organizations systemically and broadly exploit the possibilities of more flexible work schedules that telecommuting can provide. And it is common for organizations to underinvest in the support for helping people effectively integrate computerized systems into their work.

5

Worklife with Computers and Networks

This chapter examines how work with computer-based and networked systems can be organized to affect the quality of working life for clerical workers, administrative staff, professionals, and managers. A key theme and key contribution of this chapter is the analysis of specific major assumptions regarding how organizations behave—assumptions that undergird many books and articles about computerization and worklife.

Much of the research and professional literature about worklife in computerized and networked workplaces is based on a tacit assumption that organizations behave as Rational Systems. Rational Systems models emphasize formal goals, actions to achieve them, and their costs and benefits. They also tend to portray workers or managers as sharing common goals. Closed Rational Systems models focus on the rationality of organizational behavior by focusing on the participants' focus on goals and actions that are defined within a particular organizational system, such as a workgroup or organization. These models help answer questions about how computerized systems can alter idealized organizational efficiencies. But they do not provide comprehensive concepts for effectively answering questions about when people, groups and organizations will adopt specific computer and network systems, how they will use them, and what the key consequences of usage are.

A richer understanding of workplaces can be gained by relaxing the assumptions that organizations are primarily rational and closed systems. In this chapter will examine alternative assumptions. Organizations can be viewed as open systems when participants are influenced by the social relationships they have outside their immediate workplace or organization. And also examine organizations as natural systems in which participants are concerned with preserving their autonomy and the longevity of their social unit rather than simply efficiently solving work problems regardless of its consequences for them and their colleagues.

The Open Natural systems perspective can influence the "social design" of work with computerized systems, especially when those workplaces are connected by electronic networks. New computing and communications technologies increase organizational options but do not uniquely determine them. Organizational practices can shape computerization strategies as much or more than the technologies shape the organization. This chapter illustrate and contrast the implications of natural systems and rational systems assumptions for researchers and practitioners by discussing new forms of work organization, control and coordination of work, and by the integration of computing and networks into worklife.

One of the key concerns is to find ways to effectively conceptualize the relationship between new forms of computerization and changing work. Every few years systems developers and vendors champion new computer technologies which they characterize as "revolutionizing the ways that people work."

In the early 1980s, online integrated database systems were heralded as the harbingers of new forms of work. Soon, PCs and expert systems followed as the key media of transformed (and improved) worklife. In the early 1990s, groupware and networked systems have become the technological heroes for transforming worklife. During the next few years, we expect to see similar claims for multimedia, tiny computers ("personal digital assistants") and other emerging technologies.

Advocates of emerging technologies including computer scientists, technical journalists, and consultants, often characterize them as being "so fundamentally different" from their precursors that one cannot learn from previous experiences of computerization to understand some of their important uses, roles and consequences. While this position seems to recommend appropriate humility in making strong predictions, it also serves the political role of distancing a new technology from discussions about the problems that plagued some earlier information processing technologies.

Many of these technologies help managers and professionals effectively reorganize worklife. But they are less important than stories in professional magazines and the popular press suggest. Their effects are often diverse because they depend upon important contextual influences. This chapter examines some key assumptions about people, work, organizations and the roles of technologies that help us better understand the likely roles and consequences of emerging technologies.

The Importance of Work

A tacit theme in most analyses of computerization and worklife is that the quality and character of working life is an important aspect of social life. But the relevance of work quality as a major topic in the information systems field is not universally accepted. Many writers focus on the economic effects of computerization and ignore the quality of working life. The following are key reasons to believe the quality of worklife should be a central topic in discussions of computerization.

First, wage earning is a major component of many people's lives. Wage income is how most people between the ages of 22 and 65 obtain money for food, housing, clothing, transportation, etc. The United States' population is approximately 250,000,000, and well over 100,000,000 work for a living. Fundamental changes in the nature of work — the number of types of jobs, job content, career opportunities, social relations and working conditions of various kinds — affects a significant segment of society.

Second, in the United States, most wage earners work 30 - 60 hours per week — a large fraction of their waking lives. People's work experiences shape other aspects of their lives as well. Work pressures or pleasures can be carried home to families. Better jobs give people room to grow when they seek more responsible, or complex positions, while stifled careers often breed boredom and resentment in comparably motivated people. Although people vary considerably in the kinds of experiences and opportunities they want from a job, few people would be satisfied with a well paid, but monotonous, and socially isolated job.

Third, many of the arguments advanced for the economic value of new forms of computer technologies make strong tacit assumptions about how people will work with them. Understanding the relationship between computer use and organizational productivity is paramount. It is crucial to know what people's work practices and (dis)satisfactions actually are.

In the late 1980s, an array of PC-based applications commonly referred to as "productivity tools" were introduced. Most of the evidence regarding the use and value of the applications tends to be anecdotal . No extensive fine grained studies assess how this family of applications altered the productivity of the people who use them. Computer systems are regarded as expedient as shifts akin to switching from manual to power tools. The assumption is that gains in speed and effectiveness will readily accrue to most people who use these systems.

However the productivity among North American office workers during a period of intense computerization in the 1980's resulted in a period of slow growth . Productivity calculations account for the costs of buying and using technologies as well as the improvements which they offer. An observations in organizations suggest that organizations differ significantly in the extent to which they adequately train people to use computer systems, in the extent to which they encourage innovation from clerks as well as professionals, and in the extent to which the organizations learn to effectively use computing.

Fourth, computerization has had a visible direct effect on more people in their workplaces than in any other setting: home, school, church, etc. Workplaces are good places to examine how the dreams and dilemmas of computerization operate for millions of people under a variety of social and technical conditions.

One aspect of worklife that may remain problematic for analysts is the immense variety of workplaces that exist. Some researchers include organizations of diverse sizes and task orientations in their studies.

But it is always an inductive leap to generalize one's findings over a wide range of clerical, technical, professional, and managerial activities or over a wide range of manufacturing and service industries.

Rational and Natural Systems Models of Organizational Behavior

Many ideas about the function and value of computerized systems in organizations — including computerized communication systems — are strongly influenced by the conceptions of how organizations behave. It is common for many advocates and analysts of new computing and networking technologies to portray organizations as streamlined task systems. In this portrait, organizations are relatively "well oiled machines" in which jobs and worklife are well-defined. These computerized systems improve efficiencies and expand peoples' methods of efficiency. With the organization-as-machine as a background metaphor, analysts can conceptually "plug in" new families of computing and networking technologies and identify possible improvements or degradations in how people work and the ways in which organizations behave. For example, one can talk about using electronic mail (email) or telecommuting facilities to enable people to communicate more effectively while working in different places and at different times. Some go so far as to say that electronic communications "shrink time and space to zero."

The machine metaphor a one common image of organizational behavior and helps highlight the possible advantages of new computational and networking systems. But there are other important metaphors about organizational behavior. Specific organizations (or departments) have reputations as being "boiler rooms" where managers force their staffs to work hard day in and day out, while others are spoken of as "country clubs" in their ethos. There are unlikely to be many similarities of methodology in computing among "boiler rooms" and "country clubs." It is equally unlikely that computerized communication systems will be used in identical ways and with similar consequences in organizations which are primarily streamlined task systems, bureaucracies or war zones. Unfortunately, relatively few studies of computerization and worklife identify key assumptions about how organizations behave outside of the workplace under study. One key advance in this chapter is to link an understanding of computerization, work, and networking to patterns of organizational behavior which extend beyond the local workplace and workgroup.

The main problem in relying upon vivid metaphors of organizations such as machines, bureaucracies or war-zones is that they homogenize behavior within organizations. When a bank is labelled as bureaucratic because of its rigid rules in granting credit, the image of "bank as bureaucracy" paints all of the bank's behavior as similarly rule bound. It helps to have a more differentiated methodology of examining behavior in and between organizations.

Rational Systems Models of Organizational Behavior:

There are numerous models illustrating how organizations behave. Scott (1987) introduced a very helpful scheme for clustering many of these models along two key dimensions: Open Systems -Closed Systems and Rational Systems-Natural Systems.

Table 1: Rational and Natural Systems Models of Organisational Behaviour

Rational Systems	Natural Systems
Collectivities oriented toward the pursuit of relatively specific goals and exhibiting highly formalized social structures.	Collectivites whose participants share a common interest in the survival of the system and who engage in collective activites to secure this end.

In information systems development and use, computerization and worklife, and work with computer networks literature, "rational systems" models are common, and often tacit. The Rational Systems Model views organizations as instruments for specific purposes, and the most important organizational behaviors are various ways of achieving those purposes. Analysts who rely on Rational Systems Models often emphasize questions of efficiency. For example, they may ask whether CAD systems can effectively reduce the design time for a new product and whether electronic mail can efficiently substitute for face to face meetings and reduce travel costs.

When the answers to these questions focus on influences which are wholly contained within the organizational unit under study, then the model is also a Closed System model. For example, a Closed Rational analysis of a CAD system could focus on the speed, labor costs, and skills for creating designs and revising or reusing existing designs with different CAD systems (or manually). However, other answers to the same set of questions might focus on relationships between the groups that use CAD and groups that are outside of their organization.

Table 2: Closed Versus Open Systems Models of Organisation

Closed Systems	Open Systems
All key influences on organizational behavior come from within the identified organization	Some key influences on organisational behaviour come from outside the identified organisatopm—through relationships with clients, suppliers, other institutions such as schools, regulatory bodies, progessional associations, etc.

For example, one CAD system may make it easier to exchange design data with a major customer while another otherwise similar CAD package may accept more industry standard formats and thus help the designers work efficiently with more new customers. These relationships between customers in one set of organizations and people who use CAD in another organization are part of an open-systems analysis.

The best known Open Rational Systems models of organization-level behavior are the "contingency models" which hold that the best way to organize depends upon key features of an organization's "environment." Contingency analysts would argue that organizations which are making products and delivering services in relatively stable environments can be most effectively organized with highly refined systems of rules and sharp divisions of labor.

In contrast, organizations which have dynamic markets for their products and services are most effective when they are organized in less bureaucratic ways. In practice, organizations may mix their level of bureaucratization. This line of theorizing helps explain why universities may have highly centralized control over new courses and curricula (through faculty committees) while having relatively high levels of decentralization in opening up new lines of research when they are initiated by individual faculty.

Closed Rational System models do not provide strong concepts for understanding ambiguity in the kinds of problems facing organizational participants, their goals, lines of action, available means, value of specific technologies, the best ways of organizing work, etc. The Closed Rational Systems models are often used to help answer questions about the efficiency and effectiveness of organizational methods, the value of new technologies, etc. Many research studies of electronic communications focus on these kinds of questions, including:

What is the effect of electronic media on communication efficiency, participation, and interpersonal behavior? Which features are most important to people who use specific computer systems? How can a communication medium be selected to most effectively match the communication task?

Closed Rational systems model the men and women who use computers as selecting equipment which is most suitable for their current tasks and using it efficiently for those tasks. Open Rational systems models examine how people and organizations select and use computing equipment in ways that are influenced by social relationships which extend outside their focal organization as well as by technical requirements which are shaped by their tasks and social relationships within their home organizations. For example, a Closed Rational systems analysis cannot account for the possibility that people often want to use computer systems which can help them qualify for better jobs in another organization. In contrast, Open systems models can accommodate such relationships (ie, possible future employers) who are located outside of the person's home organization. Similarly, an Open Rational systems analysis of electronic mail use would ask what sorts of social relationships outside of the focal organization influence a person's interest in using electronic communication and activities that she uses it for. An engineer may argue that she needs access to the Internet in order to track professional events on comp.software-engineering, but may actually find other bulletin boards which focus on recreation (rec.*) even more interesting and time- consuming. The Open Rational systems models have rarely been applied in research studies of computerization and work with networks.

Professionals and managers try to understand the economic dimensions of computing and networks. However, the reliance on Closed Rational systems models of economic and organizational behavior leaves out important aspects of worklife with computing that practitioners should not ignore when they seek reliable analyses.

Natural Systems Models of Organizational Behavior:

Natural Systems models are one major alternative to rational systems models of organizations. There is an interesting body of sociological research which shows that organizational members often develop new purposes to keep an organization going, even when original goals were met or at least resolved. Many of the key members may have a stake in keeping the organization stable or growing. The label "natural systems" refers to the interests of organizational members in keeping their organization alive — like an organism in nature.

An interesting example of organizational activity which fits a Natural systems model is found the efforts of some centralized information systems (IS) departments to take control over as much desktop computing as they can even though many professionals and managers prefer to have local control over their systems. In the late 1980s, the upper managers of these IS departments saw their client base and their staffs shrinking, and fought to retain control over computing services in their organizations. From the viewpoint of Rational Systems models, centralized IS departments would be retained only to the extent that they could provide services more efficiently and effectively than decentralized alternatives. Moreover, their managers would also seek to organize their activities primarily in ways that would be "best" for their organizations, rather than best for the IS staff (in terms such as job security, status, pay, and influence). Natural systems theorists would predict that many IS managers would try to find ways to maintain a role for their departments even when some of these roles would advantage IS at the expense of their clients. Their efforts, in altering their mix of services and in exercising whatever political influence they could muster, would play a significant role in influencing the extent to which organizations would maintain centralized IS departments.

In Closed Natural Systems models, organizations are not as influenced by the social relationships which extend outside of their boundaries. An organization by drawing a boundary and treating the elements within that boundary as a coherent social unit oriented toward the pursuit of specific goals. If we identify the key organizational system as a particular business firm, then the efforts of its IS department to control the standards for all PC and LANs would be a closed natural system analysis.

On the other hand, some computer scientists' preference for Unix systems and related software is based on an consensus about "good computing equipment" in academic computer science, rather than on a selection of the most efficient equipment to carry out their work. If the focal unit is a specific computer science department, then this observation illustrates an Open Natural Systems analysis. Researchers have begun to examine computerization and work from the viewpoint of Open Natural Systems models. They have also begun to examine electronic communications from this perspective. Key questions that researchers have addressed recently include:

- How much are the perceived effects of electronic communications attributes of the media, and how much do they depend on the social relations that participants have with groups that extend outside their immediate workplaces?
- How can we understand the way that electronic communication can undermine face-to-face relations in work groups?
- How do different uses of computer-communications technology affect informal group processes in organizations?

Sociological theories of organizations started with Closed Rational Systems models (represented by Max Weber's model of bureaucracy and Frederick W. Taylor's analysis of scientific management) earlier in this century. In the 1930s, they expanded to include Closed Natural Systems models (the human relations school). Open Rational Systems Models (bounded rationality, contingency theory) were developed in the 1950s and 1960s, along with Open Natural Systems models (ie, negotiated order and institutional theories).

Social analysts of computerization frequently adopt similar perspectives to those of organizational theorists. In this chapter, examine how the assumptions about organizations as reflected in these four broad families of models influences were understanding of work with computing and networks. The particular theories in each of these four categories differ in some key ways, such as their levels of analysis and key organizing concepts.

The Rational System models remain influential in many practical discussions within organizations about adopting computer technology. Much of the justification given in organizations for new system purchases remains focused on tasks, equipment capabilities and costs: electronic mail, for example, may be championed because its cost per message is seen as lower than normal postal service and will provide almost-instantaneous delivery.

In contrast, Natural Systems models allows us to examine very different aspects of computerized systems. They allows professionals and managers to look beyond the "sales hype" that inevitably accompanies new technology by questioning simple cause-and-effect relationships between computer systems and work performance (i.e., technological determinism). The view from this perspective provides a broader picture of the system and its setting: hardware, software, institutions, unwritten assumptions and traditions, organizational politics — and the strengths, weaknesses, biases, personal agendas, and unpredictability of participating groups and individuals. Natural System models encourage us to examine the behavior of the organizations themselves as systems with rich political orders where important practices and structures may be institutionalized and inflexible.

Social Design of Computerized Systems and Work Settings

An exciting recent development is the effort by some researchers and practitioners to conceptualize the design of computer and networked systems as a set of interrelated decisions about technology and the organization of work. Managers and professionals who focus on the use of computing may find that this approach fits their routine practices. But thinking and talking about computerization as the development of socio-technical configurations rather than as simply installing and using a new technology is not commonplace.

Many professionals use computer technologies which expand the range of their work methods. The adoption of electronic mail to facilitate communication between people who work in different time zones and the acquisition of compact portable computers to facilitate working on the road are two routine illustrations. But organizations that adopt portable computers and email to improve the flexibility of people's work relationships must do more than simply acquire technologies to realize these specific advantages.

For example, portable computers may help people work outside of their offices. Some of the resulting convenience hinges on technological choices, such as acquiring machines which run software whose files are compatible with file formats used in the office.

But much of the resulting flexibility depends upon social choices as well. For example, if organization A requires men and women to report to work daily during regular working hours even when they have the portable computers, then people gain relatively little flexibility in work location if that policy is not also changed. People may be able to take portable computers home after hours or on weekends, or on the road while they travel.

Thus, organization A may gain some unpaid overtime work with these policies. But the men and women who work in organization A will not gain much of the "control over the location of work" which people many attribute to portable computing. In contrast, if organization B allows its employees to work at places and times which they choose, then its employees can use portable computing to have even more flexibility in their work. In each of these cases, the men and women who adopt the equipment and construct work policies and practices for organizations A and B have created distinct socio-technical configurations — or social designs. And these social designs which incorporate portable computing, rather than the technology alone, have different consequences.

In a similar way, organizations develop specific socio-technical configurations, or social designs, around electronic mail. Few organizations adopt the social design of "universal and unlimited" electronic mail access in one rapid move. Most organizations diffuse electronic mail in which some people obtain access and services more readily than others. Tacit policies about granting access to email varies from one organization to another. For example, Organization A may give email access to everyone in particular departments, while Organization B may grant mail accounts only to employees who request them.

Organizations also differ in the way that their managers construct policies related to computer communication, such as the extent to which they regulate disk space for storing mail, regulate the topics about which employees can set up computer conferences, and allow managers to monitor their subordinates email. Any collection of these kinds of policies and practices, specific email systems and their technical capabilities, and the resources to support the technology's use, form specific social designs.

Table 5: Some Elements of a Social Design

ARENA	Social Design Choices to Adopt, Create or Restructure:
Technology	Selection and configuration of hardware and software.
Social Organization of work	a. The division of labour,. b.Rewards/demands forlearning new systems. c. Access to machines and data.
Equipment Access	a. Shared vs. independent systems b. Who has access and with what privileges c. Standardization of systems and capabilities d. Extensiveness of use within a work group or organization
Infrastructure	a.Trainingprograms b. Availability of Adjunct Resources (e.g., space)
Control Patterns	a. Implementation strategy and operations b.Daily working conditions c. Levels of monitoring

The effective diffusion of mail services often takes many years in larger organizations which employ thousands of people. Even though managers may approve major equipment purchases and construct many key policies pertinent to email, many practices evolve over time.

Markus and Robey explain that computerization is often an "emergent process" whose character develops over long periods of time.

Analytical research about computerization in organizations, as well as the systematic observations, has helped us identify many arenas in which organizational participants make social choices about the socio- technical configurations of their computerized and networked systems. The term "social design of computerized systems," or "social design," to characterize the joint design of both the technological characteristics of a computerized systems and the social arrangements under which it will be used. Table 5 lists several common social dimensions which can be part of the social design of a computing or network system.

The ways in which these broad arenas are organized through explicit policies and routine practices create a structure for the opportunities and constraints of computer and network use within any organization. These "social choices" are a necessary element of computerization, even though they are usually not formally decided or completely within the control of any one actor. They can even be byproducts of oversight, such as managers who neglect to train their staffs in a new computing application because they assume that it's "just like the old one" or "very user friendly." In any organization with more than a few dozen participants, these arenas are likely to be under the control of different actors. But these "choices" can enable or hinder the actual role of new technologies in changing work. Consequently, system developers and managers can support or subvert the possible advantages of "better technologies" through their social designs, even when they are implicit.

The social consequences of computerization or network use are dependent on the choices in these arenas, as well as other similar ones. The particular collection of social design choices can vary from one organization to another, and even often within organizations. When managers and professionals adopt or enhance a new computerized system, they may be able to alter some of these practices (and policies).

The social design of work systems with computing does not necessarily improve the quality of peoples' work lives. For example, some managers have computerized relatively routinized clerical work by fragmenting jobs and tightening supervisors' abilities to monitor the quality, pace and speed of people's work. These same managers may develop good systematic training programs for the clerks whose work is now more regimented. However, social design can also be very benign. It encourages participants in a computerization project to review the web of practices and policies related to computing which can otherwise be "unanticipated."

UC Irvine's faculty, staff, and students use several different mail systems, and sending files across them is not always seamless. The person who wants to reliably manage memos that flow between these diverse mail systems need more sophisticated skills (or staff support) than do those people who communicate primarily within only one of these systems.

The assumptions that seem to shape the Vice Chancellor's conception of a memo system focuses upon the distributors and their resources. His email message does not ask whether the faculty, staff and students who receive electronic memos have an adequate infrastructure for supporting their management.

The Vice Chancellor may view his proposed distribution system as simply exploiting existing computing resources. However it is an implicit social design because it reshapes work with computing.

The collection of email networks at UCI is not a single artifact. Its technical architecture includes several mail systems and gateways, dozens of computers which run several operating systems, thousands of diverse microcomputers and workstations, and numerous diverse printers.

Technical support comes from several different organizational locations. Control of technical resources such as disk space and printers often lies outside the immediate administrative domain of faculty, staff or students.

The overall system, including administrative controls for authenticating distributions at one end, and for assuring trustworthy receipt and management, is itself a complex socio-technical organization. And the "memo management systems" would be intricately woven into a rich web of social relationships which couple administrative authority, rules for obedience to the directives of some memos, the allocation of computing resources, and numerous new practices.

Most explicit social d esign approaches would have lead analysts in this situation to examine the process and organization of work for producing, distributing, receiving, reading and managing memos rather than focussing primarily upon one stage. However, different approaches to social design would conceptualize the key elements of that design very differently.

Use of E-Mail for Internal Communication

Mail and Records Services has developed a new "master distribution" system with the help of Academic Computing and Network and Telecommunications. This system will allow us to significantly reduce paper use and costs associated with printing and delivering distributions. Individuals with on-line access to E-Mail will now receive most distributions electronically. Those without on-line access will continue to receive paper copies.

Two of the major approaches to social design contrast strongly in their assumptions about people, organizations, technology and work. Business Process Reengineering is usually applied by managers and consultants to streamline operations. The main aims of these reengineering projects seem to be reducing the time for a specific business process, such as dispatching a repairman to a site or processing an insurance claim, and also reducing the number of people who work on that activity. However, some consultants have promised more diverse financial benefits to their clients (and potential clients).

Figure 1: Announcing an Electronic Memo Distribution System

David Schnitt (1993) characterizes a business process in these terms:

> A business process is best defined as an activity in the organization fundamental to operating the business that serves an internal or external customer and has a well-defined outcome or series of

> outcomes. Every organization is made up of business processes. Examples include such mundane activities as accounts payable, inventory control, field service, or the processing of a customer application (such as in a bank or insurance company), but also includes less "back office" and more "front-office" processes such as new product development and budgeting. Since many work steps in business processes are executed by people in different departments, this view encourages a cross-functional perspective....the business process view of the Accounts Payable (A/P) process sheds new light on it as a complicated, slow, error-prone process involving many different departments and personnel. It reveals that the process is really the procurement process, not just A/P. Seen from this perspective, the opportunities for improvement are much greater. The key is to focus on the value-added outcome of the process (why it is done, not what is done) and how it relates to other processes in the organization. (Schnitt, 1993)

Michael Thomas (1993) describes business process reengineering in these terms:

> The central message of reengineering is that business processes are generally built around paper, a technology with drawbacks that are obvious in a business environment. Technologies such as electronic imaging allow information to be located and communicated instantaneously, to be viewed simultaneously, to be acted upon in real time, often with the customer right on the phone. Blessed with such power, organizations can cast off procedures that are geared toward paper, often with dramatic results.

Business process reengineering brings an industrial engineering perspective to the design of organizations and work. The flow of documents and authorizations are key elements, and the character of people's jobs is a secondary consideration in much of the writing about this approach to redesigning organizations. Computer systems of various kinds are often key elements of a reengineering project, including scanners and document processing systems at the "front end" of a process, and the use of workflow software to model and mange some of the subsequent activity.

The analyses which support these projects usually rest on Rational systems models of organizations. They can be Open Rational systems models when they examine workflows that run across departments. But they are usually closed off at organizational boundaries, except to view services from the viewpoint of cstomers/clients. They usually examine few influences on worklife and work organization other than those that directly pertain to reliable and efficient workflows.

The major alternative approach, sometimes called socio-technical systems design, makes people and their relationships in support of work, rather than workflows, the center of organizational reforms with information technology. Peter Keen articulates this approach in these terms:

> The business team, rather than the functionally defined hierarchy or the dotted-line or matrix-management variants that show up on the organization chart, is increasingly being seen as the real unit of organizing. Business is finally recognizing that division of labor is increasingly ineffective as the basis for an organization in an

> environment of constant rather than occasional change and of shifting functions to the proven project and team-based processes long employed by the research and technical functions. Teamwork is relational; the quality of performance rests on the quality of interactions, communication, and coordination among team members.
>
> Information technology affords the opportunity to build what might be termed the "relational" organization: an organization defined not by fixed structures but by ease of relationships. Instead of focusing on organization structure, business today needs to look at the mechanisms that make communication simple, flexible...IT makes practical many of the visions of management thinkers. The management principles for exploiting IT organizational advantage require a basic rethinking of old assumptions—especially concerning the links between strategy and structure—at the top of the firm.
>
> Flexibility and adaptability are the new watchwords for organizations and for people. Firms that do not attend to their people's careers as well as their jobs might well have to replace much of their work force. Their human capital will be a depreciated resource, one they may find harder to replenish than they thought.

Keen's analysis appeals to many professionals. One technologically oriented corollary leads some computer scientists to develop designs for computer systems which facilitate communication and collaboration in diverse forms: mail systems, conferencing systems, co-authoring systems, and so on. But it is much too facile to think that lower status workers, such as clerks and semi-professionals are most appropriately targeted with business process reengineering while only higher status workers, such as managers and professionals, can bask in a more supportive and enriched relational organization.

For example, Jim Euchner and Patricia Sachs recently reported about the redesign of a "work system" in which a regional U.S. phone company (NYNEX) provided customers with high speed (T.1) phone service. The installation required the collaboration of over 40 people in 5 distinct departments, NYNEX took much longer to complete these installations than their competitors, and rapidly lost significant market share in New York City. A computerized scheduling system had been used to assign different technicians to their specialized activities in the installation and fine-tuning of the T.1 lines in customers' offices. A large part of the delay seemed to derive from the way that some key problems cut across the domains of different technicians — they were either problems at system interfaces, or problems whose causes were somewhat ambiguous. The computer system helped to efficiently schedule the technicians' trips to the site — one at a time — to give them full and balanced workloads. It did not help bring together the specific technicians who would be needed to solve the more vexing installation problems.

A group from NYNEX's Science and Technology Center collaborated in a socio-technical design with both the craft workers and managers who were responsible for T.1 installations to develop a new "work system design." Some of the principles of work system design that they articulated are common themes in many socio-technical systems projects. For example, they had craft workers who do the actual work, as well as more senior managers, design the new work system and implement it. They focussed on workflows and whole processes rather than upon discrete tasks, a concept which is shared with many business process reengineering projects.

However, they sought to provide people with ownership and responsibility for whole jobs, rather than discrete tasks. And they developed some specific guidelines for designing computer and communication systems: to support workflows and communications; to provide "intelligent" information handling; and to have interfaces that match the language in which people conceptualize their work.

The new T.1 work system reorganized the installations around cross-functional teams who have joint responsibility for insuring that installations are prompt and effective. The team's composition is rather fluid and can depend upon the specific customer and the stage of the installation. But they usually mix both white collar and blue collar workers, and can include people at different managerial levels. The coordination relies upon people scheduling technicians rather than upon computerized scheduling, although computer support is provided for other activities. In this particular case, the work system was redesigned, while the existing computer systems were left untouched.

Jewett and Kling report the case of a pharmaceutical firm in which sales managers radically restructured the responsibilities of sales clerks from passive order-takers to be more proactive sales representatives. The department held extensive meetings to reconceptualize their roles, and the staff rewrote all of the job descriptions. The resulting jobs were enriched and also reclassified at somewhat higher pay levels. The department's managers also commissioned the development of a new computerized information system to provide richer searching capabilities to support the restructured jobs. In this case, the configuration of the information systems was part of a larger social design which included the explicit reconceptualization of key jobs.

These socio-technical strategies require that systems analysts and designers understand many of the work practices, schedules, resource constraints, and other contingencies of the people who will use the new computerized systems. Some organizations, such as NYNEX, have included social scientists on their design teams to facilitate such observation and understanding. They also recommend that people who use the systems have a substantial role in specifying their designs as well as altered work practices. One reason that stand-alone microcomputers may have been so attractive for many people is that they offered more control over the form of computerization and changes in work than systems which ran on shared computer systems. In addition, microcomputer users' work methods made them less dependent upon having access to busy full time computer professionals to design and modify systems. This made their computing arrangements more adaptable. Many organizations implemented PC systems with a tacit social design that gave their workers more autonomy.

A third approach to social design is congruent with both business process reengineering and socio-technical design: web analyses of computing infrastructure. One key insight of this approach is that social designs which focus primarily on the overt work system, such as processing an insurance claim or installing a phone line, can overlook the kinds of systems and support which are critical for making computer and communications systems workable for people. For example, in a study of computing and organizational practices in a large number of leading companies, McKersie and Walton observe, "Despite widespread recognition among IT planners that most systems are underutilized because of inadequate training, the deficiency is repeated in systems implementation after systems implementation."

Training is only one element of infrastructure for computing support. The computing infrastructure in a subsequent section of this chapter. Web analysis locates computer systems and people who use them in a matrix relationships with other people, organizations and technologies on which they depend. Kling provides concrete criteria to help analysts draw larger boundaries around computer and work systems, so that one can examine how they actually work and how they can effectively be changed and sustained. Identifying relevant infrastructure is one part of a web analysis. Identifying other resources, such as data sources and participants' incentives for supporting a work system, is also part of the analysis. When these resources cross administrative or organizational boundaries they are excluded from many systems analyses. Web analyses help social designers include them explicitly.

There are two key observations. First, computing infrastructure can play a key role in social designs. A group may prefer a high performance computing application which requires substantial training and consulting, or a medium performance application which people may learn more effectively on their own.

Whichever application is chosen makes subsequent demands upon computing infrastructure for those work groups. Organizations often fail to realize the gains from IT that they hope for when they: a) select high performance applications and fail to provide needed support or training in their use; or b) select lower performance applications but still do not encourage people to experiment and learn in their workplaces.

Business process reengineering often rests upon Rational Systems models. Since one overt goal of many of these projects is reducing the number of people employed in an area (often referred to as "downsizing" or "decapitation"), it should not be very surprising that the people who will do redesigned work are often unenthusiastic about sharing their best insights with designers. Natural Systems models of organizations take much more explicit account of people's social behavior (such as seeking occupational security, careers, and specific kinds of economic and social rewards from work). Natural systems models underlie many of the socio-technical design projects. Closed Natural systems models might help understand what a redesigned work system should look like. But Closed Natural system models are not sufficiently rich to help understand how readily a new social design can be implemented.

New Forms of Work Organization

To what extent do new computing and communication technologies foster new forms of work? Many writers, including scholars, professionals and technical journalists, have speculated about the effects of new technologies on work life. These speculations are often based on tacitly-held models of organizational behavior. For example, an analyst viewing organizations from a Rational Systems perspective may speculate that electronic mail will eliminate organizational hierarchies, or at least reduce the barriers to communication between people at different levels of hierarchy in an organization. From the same perspective, electronic communications may facilitate the formation of more flexible work groups (perhaps even "virtual" work groups). From a human relations perspective — a Closed Natural systems model — one might predict that new forms of computerization would create novel possibilities for organizational learning.

Other speculations involve the extent and the conditions under which electronic communications will foster or undermine a sense of community in the workplace and elsewhere. Workers who are connected by electronic communications media may form "communities" that differ in substantial ways from other communities to which they may belong. Much of what has been written about networks at work has been concerned, in part, with community. A recurring theme of electronically-enhanced group cohesion is typified by Heintz, who claims that "the world of electronic science is smaller and more tightly knit." This theme tacitly emphasizes the tight relationship of technology and tasks which one finds in Rational Systems Models of organizations. Unfortunately, there are currently few empirical studies of changing forms of work which support these speculations. Technical journalists like Perry claim that "electronic mail has removed the barriers of time and place between engineers collaborating on complex design projects."

Aydin and Rice describe how networks bring together different groups in the workplace. There is some empirical evidence that computer nets help foster electronic communities among geographically or organizationally isolated professionals, such as special librarians and oceanographers. However, professionals who are already busy with strong professional relationships and nearby colleagues may be much less likely to participate in these semi-public forums.

The most active researchers in certain areas of computer science rarely post messages on publicly available Internet bulletin boards devoted to specialized topics, including comp.groupware, comp.software-engineering, comp.society and comp.infosystems. One can't infer patterns of participation from a simple Rational Systems description of a task, such as "communicating with colleagues."

But there is also the possibility that people's social relationships in networked offices may suffer in some ways. Research claims about email facilitating less inhibited behavior and flaming suggest that electronic groups may work somewhat differently than face-to-face groups. Kezsbom, a technical journalist, suggests one possible down-side to networked worklife: "As the use of cross-functional, multi-disciplined project teams increases, the conflict that accompanies such team work will rise accordingly."

Markus describes an organization in which electronic mail is often used to avoid face-to-face confrontation or unpleasant situations, and in which in-office visitors are ignored while employees tend to the demands of messages on their computer terminals. And Zuboff reports on a large drug company where managers claimed that their electronic communications were being treated as policy statements, even when they wanted to make an informal observation or ad-hoc decisions.

One recurring theme in this debate, typified by studies of scientists using networks, is the nature of the social relationships and "community feelings" that develop in electronic groups. These groups are diverse. They differ in dimensions like place (same vs different), size of group, and how open or closed participation is (tightly defined project teams vs. discussion groups who are open to all who have accounts on a particular network).

Electronic work groups vary widely and behaviors in groups with one set of characteristics may not be important in groups with very different structural characteristics. Small, local closed groups where people also have common face to face meetings may behave very differently than large, open groups where most participants have never met each other and where group norms are developed on-line.

In this section, will examine the impact of computers and communications on intact work groups — those in which the employees work in close physical proximity to each other on a daily basis. This section also will examine the complexities that arise as communication technologies are applied to distributed groups — those in which individuals and groups are connected primarily by electronic media, either on the job or in other professional or recreational activities.

Intact Work Groups

A group's non-electronic interaction is part of the "glue" which holds the group together. Intact groups often have more in common than simple face-to-face workplace contact: as members of an office, they may participate in parties or other group-sponsored social events that would increase their sense of community. For members of a scientific community, periodic participation in conferences may encourage or reinforce a sense of community, even when their daily communication is solely by electronic means.

Electronic communications can change the static concept of associations within the workplace. Sproull and Kiesler, describing the second-level, or social, effects of new communications technologies, find that people now "pay attention to different things, have contact with different people, and depend on one another differently." In much the same way as a person may assume different roles outside the workplace (husband/wife, father/mother, golf partner, churchgoer), the same person may now assume different (electronic) roles — simultaneously — within the workplace. Several new or expanded roles may be facilitated by electronic communications, such as active professional specialty development or participation in work-related task forces or project activity. Analyses which consider this type of change in work life go beyond the Rational Systems perspective to show "emergent" behavior of groups that use electronic mail. As this behavior evolves with technological changes, the tasks that a person performs become less stable, and the mix of tasks within a group shift in ways that are best explained by Natural Systems Models.

One of the most intriguing and popular conceptualizations of the potential impact of computing technology on work life is Zuboff's distinction between automating work and informating work.

To "automate" is to replace human activity with a machine (computer) which is faster, more reliable, more subject to control, etc. The typical goals of automation "have typically been those of cost reduction, efficiency, and productivity. .... Automation ...means applying technology in ways that increase the self acting and self regulating capacities of machine systems, thus minimizing human intervention.

Intelligent technology can be used to automate, but even as this occurs, the technology has the capacity to translate those automated activities into data and to display those data. Information technology symbolically renders processes, objects, behaviors and events so that they become visible, knowable and sharable in a new way." ... This second function is 'informate.' 'To informate' means to translate and make visible; 'informating' occurs as processes, objects, behaviors and events are translated and made visible as explicit information....

Under these conditions, 'to work' becomes more abstract, since it depends upon an understanding of, responsiveness to, and ability to manage and create value from information. In an informated environment, skills are refined." ... "It requires the construction of a new kind of knowledge, one that is more analytical, abstract, and conceptual....It is in terms of this second informating function that information technology represents a radical discontinuity in the history of work and the evolution of industrial technology."

Zuboff reports an intriguing case of informating in her study of an Expense Tracking System (ETS) in a paper plant. Operators in the paper plant learned about the costs of making paper from a computerized system that had been added to their existing paper making equipment. By experimenting with their equipment controls they were able to significantly reduce the costs of producing paper. The costs of chemicals and other ingredients in paper-making were previously unavailable to operators in real-time. The ETS is a great illustration of informating.

A key problem in the ETS case was the implementation process. While upper managers in the firm originally viewed the ETS as a risky project, they were pleased with the cost reductions and praised the staff involved. The managers who initiated the ETS bypassed some middle managers and worked directly with the machine operators to help give them a sense of ownership over the ETS. When the operators' results from using the ETS proved valuable to managers in corporate headquarters, these middle managers felt left out and worried about the security of their jobs. They tried to share in the glory of ETS' use by adding their names to key reports. Later they initiated policies to limit and impede operators' abilities to experiment with it. Informating the machine operators empowered them in ways that threatened their immediate managers, who in turn acted to protect their jobs and status. Themes such as worker ownership and empowerment reflect an underlying human relations (Natural Systems) perspective. However the concept of informating focusses upon the closed system of a job, information recorded about some work processes, and feedback to workers about their performance. As Zuboff shows in the ETS case, managers who are located outside of this segment of a work system can play a major role in facilitating or impeding an informating strategy.

Zuboff's distinction between informating and automating has become the center of significant attention and unpublished controversy. Her catchy and vivid imagery has stimulated some scholars to rethink their approaches to computerization. Some students like the resonance of the term "informate" because it suggests a positive and upbeat approach to computerization.

Part of Zuboff's contribution is to squarely place the analysis of computerization and work in a moral framework which values the possible innovations from all workers, including clerks and production workers. And Zuboff's case studies provide vivid testimony to the ways that many managers are frightened of tapping the creative potential of their workers, and thus also risking a loss of their own authority and power. Informating is a great buzzword. Unfortunately, it is hard to identify how many kinds of work could be effectively informated based on Zuboff's particular definition. For example, how would one informate the job of a person who is word processing legal contracts? Zuboff's conceptualization of informating seems to have been inspired by "closed loop" process control systems where blue collar workers can become more analytical when they obtain data (and training) to help them monitor and analyze their own work.

The moral force of informating derives from the use of new technologies and reconceptualized work to empower and ennoble workers. Her conception of informating focusses on people and their work in isolation, even though empowerment tacitly refers to social relationships which extend outside of a particular workgroup. Like other Closed Natural systems analyses, the informating concept isn't rich enough to help us understand when organizations will experiment with new forms of work — or when these experiments will be successfully sustained over a period of time (and when they will be quickly abandoned). This is a common conceptual limitation of many Closed systems analyses. By adopting the broader perspective of Open Natural Systems models, the analyst can better account for the negotiations and power relationships between the focal group and the diverse outside groups and people with whom they interact.

Distributed Groups

Many of the speculations about the impact of computers and communication technologies involve the ability of these technologies to facilitate new forms of work organization that are not limited solely to the traditional, integral work place. As these technologies become an increasingly important part of work life, and proliferate even into the home, some writers examined the unique characteristics of the media themselves, and predicted both positive and negative effects which might result from using the new media. Other writers predicted — and in many cases strongly advocated — that electronic communications be used to restructure the traditional social organization of work into such new forms as distributed work groups, telecommuting, and special-interest (possibly non-work-related) groups.

Media and Communications

A substantial body of research has attempted to identify the unique characteristics of electronic media, and how new media use may be optimized. While much of this research is social-psychological in nature, a few researchers engage issues of organizational behavior. Kiesler, Siegel, and McGuire conducted controlled problem- solving experiments which compared computer-based communication with face-to-face discussion. They found that the groups that used computer-communication took longer to reach consensus, participated more equally, showed higher choice shift, and displayed more "uninhibited verbal behavior" (colloquially known as "flaming").

Additional studies by this widely-recognized, pioneering research group, which support and expand these findings, are presented in Kiesler, et.al and in Sproull and Kiesler. Some of the effects which they observed have been attributed to the absence of non-verbal cues which are present in face-to-face discussion (body language, smiles or frowns, etc.) and even to some extent in telephone conversation (laughter, voice inflection, etc.).

Several investigators have contested the view of email as a medium which alters social behavior because it reduces social cues about other people's social roles and emotional responses. Markus challenges the rational "cues filtered out" theory, and concludes from case study evidence that managers ascribe negative effects of electronic communications to "people's deliberately intended inappropriate behavior." The negative effects that she cited were primarily focused on depersonalization — including employee feelings that the company was a less personal place to work, feelings of "invisibility," reduced feedback on job performance, and avoidance of personal contact. She believes that in some cases, these negative effects occur as ironic byproducts of people's attempts to avoid potential problems with system use. Lea and his associates have also re-examined much of the literature on "flaming" in electronic mail. They re-interpret the evidence to suggest that flaming is much less widespread than has been reported, and that it is very much dependent on the context in which the systems are used. Lea suggests that if flaming depended only upon using email, then people should flame at comparable rates on all bulletin boards, including all of those on Usenet/Internet. However, they observe that flaming is relatively common on some Usenet/Internet boards and comparatively rare on others. Something other than "email use" and "cueless media" must be invoked to explain these differences.

The systematic study of media effects pre-dates the emergence of email and was initiated to help understand the role of telephones in personal communication. The research was extended by scholars like Short, Williams, and Christie, who compared face-to-face conferences with audio-only and audio-plus-video techniques. Ronald Rice has examined the tasks which are most appropriate for a wide range of new media. One key finding is that richer media (e.g., video conferencing) are more suited to less analyzable tasks, while less rich media (e.g., electronic mail) are appropriate for more analyzable tasks. Although these findings are useful in many situations, they are based on a Rational Systems model of organizations.

To illustrate the difference between Rational and Natural Systems perspectives, it will contrast a recent technical press description of the latest "groupware" software packages with a careful study of actual groupware use in a prestigious organization. In a PC Magazine sidebar, Ulanoff offers a choice of groupware for five types of work groups (with catchy names such as the "worn-sneakers" group) and suggests which software packages will meet the needs of each group. On the other hand, Orlikowski illustrates a situation in which the

Chief Information Officer (CIO) of a large international consulting firm carefully chose a new groupware package (Lotus Notes), but failed to implement an incentive structure that encouraged its use. The CIO expected consultants to share case reports about common consulting issues with their colleagues in other offices. He believed that the consultants would use Lotus Notes to learn from each other, and to save time if they encountered a problem that had already been solved in another location. But the consultants' incentive structure was based on having "billable time" from clients for each of their activities. The firm's managers failed to modify this incentive structure. The consultants had no way to bill the significant amount of time for learning to use the new software or time that they would spend writing case reports that might help another consultant in another office. An analyst using a Natural Systems perspective could have recognized in advance the conflict between the assumed incentives and the incentives that were actually in place. The resulting explicit social design then could have included, for example, a company-wide "overhead" fund for the new work tasks that consultants would perform with the new software.

A Rational Systems assumption of the related "media richness" and "cues filtered out" theories is that communication between employees — by whatever media — will always be focused on task-related topics. From a Natural Systems perspective this is not likely to be the case. A recent study of office life found that a large percentage of employees report spending many of their working hours in non-work-related conversations and activities. Suppose, for example, that an employee enters the office one Monday morning wearing a cast on his leg. If the same employee interacted with his colleagues only by electronic media, the cast would be effectively invisible. But in a face-to-face setting, this non-task-related cue would almost certainly become the focus of conversation: "What happened?" ... "Ski accident" ... and so on. Many other non- task-related cues could have a similar effect: the sudden appearance (or disappearance) of a wedding ring, or even a new hair style or color.

Natural Systems models are needed for analysts to understand this behavior, to evaluate the practical differences between electronic media and other forms of communication in the workplace, and to develop social designs which accommodate non-task-related as well as task-related activities.

Distributed Work Groups

One major change in work organization following the introduction of electronic mail and other new communications technologies is the formation of new, geographically-distributed work groups. Although there are few systematic studies of these groups, there are numerous accounts which point to their growing importance. These groups may be short-lived, with a specific one-time task to perform such as a new product design. They may also be ongoing and broad-purposed, as in the case of the Tandem Corporation where 10,000 field service engineers use a particular bulletin board to discuss technical problems. "Electronic teams" may also extend in membership beyond the boundaries of a single corporation or university: one of the first and most famous interorganizational electronic teams was formed to develop the Common LISP programming language.

Steele claims that the design of the Common LISP programming language project would not have been possible without electronic mail to facilitate communication between hundreds of computer scientists in numerous organizations around the globe. Many other published examples of distributed work groups are primarily engineering teams in high-technology firms such as Digital Equipment, Hewlett-Packard, and Sun Microsystems.

Perry's focus, like that of many other writers, is on the contribution of electronic communication systems to specific job task performance. This focus assumes a Rational Systems Model of the organizations that use the new technologies. From this perspective, many of the features that Perry ascribes to electronic mail systems are impressive: for example, the ability to send help requests to 10,000 people simultaneously, the round-the-clock work structure of design teams that span global time zones, and the easing of language barriers in a U.S.-Russian design collaboration.

Both Perry and Sproull and Kiesler also list some "down sides" of electronic mail, including the impact of a 10,000-copy request on the 9,985 addressees who do not have an answer, or for whom the question is irrelevant. But as in intact work groups, the emergent natural phenomena of electronically-connected distributed work group behavior may be far more complex than a listing of "advantages versus disadvantages" can reveal. The Open Natural Systems perspective can also enrich understanding of distributed work groups. One example of an issue that an analyst might consider is the impact of new group structures on career lines and promotion opportunities for group members.

In the Tandem Computer illustration, one could examine the incentives for field engineers to spend time helping the peers in other parts of the world, rather than spending the same time with their own customers and peers in their office in face-to-face contact. An implicit social design, for example, might base their promotion on some reported measure of customer satisfaction, thus limiting their enthusiasm for helping remote colleagues. An explicit social design could look beyond the person and the specific task-oriented group, to recognize and reward collaborative behavior.

Telecommuting

Telecommuting is one of the most misunderstood phenomena related to work with networks. Futurists like Alvin Toffler have been enamored with the possibility that people who commute to a collective office could elect to work at home. In The Third Wave, Toffler portrayed homes with computer and communications equipment for work as "electronic cottages". This concept, with labels like "telecommuting" and "telework," have been the subject of numerous studies..

Some writers speculate that richer multimedia information systems, such as those supported by Integrated Services Digital Network (ISDN), may lead to more telecommuting because they would support more effective conferencing. But managers often computerize work with several competing logics, in which conferencing ability may be only a subordinate consideration. They may be concerned with maintaining some control over their subordinates' time and pay, but also with allowing sufficient flexibility and self-direction to insure quality work and retain good employees. Certain organizations may pay less but attempt to offer attractive working conditions — one of which could be to allow full time workers to work at home part of the work week. This is relatively rare because of the problems created with workplace control, although many self-employed people do work at home.

The possibility of firms giving employees computer equipment to use at home while communicating with their offices via electronic mail opens up many possibilities. Working at home might decrease urban traffic congestion during commuting hours, give parents more opportunity for contact with young children, and allow people to spend more time in their neighborhoods. However, people who work a substantial fraction of the time at home may be unavailable for meetings with colleagues, less visible to their peers and (therefore) passed over for promotions, and would be difficult to supervise unless they worked on a piece-rate system. Some people may lack sufficient self-discipline for work at home. Managers and researchers should consider how well electronic community-building via computer networks can compensate for loss of the traditional workplace community.

Popular accounts frequently claim that home may be a less distracting place to work than the collective office. Closed Rational Systems assumptions underlie this claim, as that model leads one to examine only the worker (in isolation) and the specific job tasks to be performed. Experience has taught us that home is a different kind of place to work — with its own privacies and problems. Homeworkers report a different set of attractions and distractions at home: sociable neighbors may expect to be able to drop in any time; children returning from school demand attention in the middle of the afternoon, the refrigerator may beckon others too frequently, and so on. Some parents choose to work at home because they can spend time with their babies and pre-school children, but they often accomplish less than at their traditional offices.

Olson's study of full time work at home by computer professionals exemplifies some of the empirical studies. She found reduced job satisfaction, reduced organizational commitment and higher role conflict in her sample. She also wonders whether work-at-home practices can exacerbate workaholism. These reports may be puzzling unless one looks beyond a Closed Rational explanation to an Open Natural understanding that is more congruent with the telecommuter's actual activities.

Forester recently critiqued the visions of full-time work at home via telecommuting as a romantic preference. After coming to appreciate the social isolation reported by several people who worked at home full time, he speculated that many of the most ardent advocates of full time work at home with computing have never done it themselves. Whether organizations will allow substantial fractions of their workforce to work at home with computing part time (1-3 days a week), for reasons of personal flexibility or to reduce commuting remains an open question. Few homes are designed for efficient home offices, and there are many important questions about the pros and cons of part time work-at-home with computing (and fax) for those who prefer this option.

A few organizations have conducted limited pilot tests of telecommuting. But these organizations and others keep the majority of their desk-bound work force keystroking in the office rather than at home. Workers may be given computer equipment to use for unpaid overtime work. To date, however, no large firms have dispersed a large fraction of their full-time work force to their homes or even satellite work centers to work with computer systems. Members of a few professions, such as journalists, professors, salesmen, and accountants take notebook computers on the road when they travel.

The desire to maintain control underlies many managers' fears of having their employees work full-time at home. It is easier for managers to ensure that people are putting in a fair day's work in an office from nine to five, than to work out elaborate contracts about the work to be done each week or month. This is an implicit social design, which emphasizes control. Employees may have different fears, such as reduced promotion opportunities that may result from lack of personal contact with managers. Further, office workers often find it easier to coordinate with people who are often wanted for meetings if they are in their collective offices. Work at home increases tensions about control over work. This is most evident when high technology firms, whose marketers promote the visions of bountiful technology for all, refuse to let a significant fraction of their professionals work at home part time as an alternative to the daily grind of urban commuting. An explicit social design which accommodates the interests of both management and employees could facilitate change in ways which technology also has so far failed to do.

Distributed Common-Interest Groups

Electronically-connected groups are not limited to those within a single workplace or to those within a single (possibly geographically dispersed) organization; nor are they limited to those with a single, narrow task focus. A more open-ended group may be composed of people with common professional interests or specialties, separated by geography but using electronic mail or bulletin boards to maintain contact. An illustrative case is that of special librarians — experts in a very specific (and perhaps narrow) field of research literature — each of whom is a library's only specialist in that field. Ladner and Tillman have found that these people rely heavily on electronic communications to link them with others in their own specialties. Oceanographers are among the many scientific communities who have specialized electronic network support available to them. One intriguing aspect of these groups is that they allow their participants the opportunity to develop their own culture, distinct from the culture of the workplace, as Tom Finholt and Lee Sproull found in a recent study.

Even people with little or no common work tasks or professional interests may participate in electronic groups in the pursuit of hobbies, recreation, or social contacts. People have traditionally formed social clubs — ranging from formally organized and structured associations to loose, ad-hoc gatherings — that are centered around common interests such as hiking, sports, movies, and the like. Today, similar groups may form around electronic bulletin board activity — forums which may be as simple as a local "dial up" number for exchanging information about a single computer game or as complex as the nearly 2000 topics available to Internet subscribers worldwide.

For any of these groups, the number of core participants may be an important factor in sustaining group activity — there may be a minimum number of regular contributors below which the group may cease to function. Markus made a major contribution to the understanding of electronic communication by examining the extent to which some minimal fraction of a social unit's members, "a critical mass," must be available via email for many people to find it useful. Markus articulated a simple critical mass model in which connectivity must be "all or nothing"; that is, all members of a group must be electronically connected in order for the group to function through the electronic medium. While this criterion is idealized, it helps Markus show how sustained electronic group behavior is a community-level phenomenon.

Markus focussed on email, but her critical mass theory also applies to interest groups which communicate via distribution lists and bulletin boards. For example, the committee members of a professional society may attempt to use a distribution list to conduct some of their business. Unless most of the committee's members use email regularly, the electronic forum will not function very well. Markus' observations also extend to bulletin boards where participation is voluntary, such as those on the Internet.

Special-interest electronic groups may support the normal interests and activities of a work place or they may cause conflict. Zuboff studied an organization in which a group of about 130 professional women formed a private electronic conference that threatened male managers. This case is particularly illustrative of the explanatory power of Open Natural Systems models, since it involves activities that were conducted in the workplace but addressed subject material — in this case, women's issues — that are much broader in scope than simple work-task performance. Participation in this group was discouraged by upper managers and many participants dropped out. Managers may not have explicitly considered themselves as censors. But their implicit social design of this aspect of the work setting nevertheless contained a strong element of censorship. It would not be surprising if electronic communications systems are used in practice primarily to form groups that upper managers deem to be safe, except in those special organizations — like universities and R&D labs — where there are strong norms against censorship.

Speculations about the possibility of computerization fostering new forms of work organization may be very engaging. Enthusiasts of the position that computerization can lead to new forms of work have the advantage of offering exciting possibilities. However, they rarely face the complexities of social control which are central in Natural Systems models.

Control, Coordination and Cooperation in Electronic Workplaces

The models of organizational behavior which presented thus far illustrate two important dimensions along which analysts may inform their explanations of the changes which accompany the introduction of new technology in the workplace. But although models in each quadrant of organizing table share many basic assumptions, each quadrant also includes a whole family of models which may differ substantially along dimensions other than open/closed or rational/natural. One example of a separate dimension which characterize analytical perspectives is that of control versus cooperation. Analysts who see organizational conflict as chronic, cooperation as bounded and patterns of control as often in contention, are likely to share a Natural Systems perspective.

At one extreme, the Neo-Marxist perspective divides people who work into two broad categories: owners and their managerial representatives on the one hand, and workers of various kinds on the other. Neo-Marxists assume that these two classes have very strong conflicting interests, and that class-conflict is the primary basis for workplace conflicts. An influential analyst, Harry Braverman, argued that the logic of capitalism requires owners and managers to relentlessly enhance their control over workers to reduce labor costs. Braverman's theory has been influential in shaping critical studies of technology in worklife. In the images of Mowshowitz and Perrolle (which follow Braverman's argument), managers computerize so as to tighten control at every turn. Braverman's theorizing has the advantage of analytical simplicity. It highlights important structural conflicts between managers and their subordinates which many people who write about computerization ignore. This leads analysts to focus on "bad workplaces" where people are low paid, have dead end-high pressured, repetitive jobs, and tight supervisory control, as well as "good workplaces." And there is certainly evidence that managers have developed social designs with computing where the resulting work is simplified and more tightly controlled. For example, Kraut, Dumais, and Koch report a case study of customer service representatives in a telephone company in which simplifying work was a major consequence of computerization.

But during the last decade, Braverman's labor process theory has been subject to significant criticism. Critics of Braverman's labor processes theory fault him for treating workers as purely passive agents. Further,

Braverman's theory also ignores the variety of managerial approaches for improving productivity, such as those which increase responsibility, pay and morale, rather than tightening control and de-skilling.

At the other extreme are Rational Systems analysts who assume that cooperation, rather than control, is the dominant element in work groups. These analysts are often interested in developing software to enhance cooperation within and between groups. However, they often assume that technologies labelled as "computer support for cooperative work" will usually be used in cooperative workgroups and that elegant groupware will readily improve a work group's performance.

Although both extremes to be overstated, the issue of control and cooperation is one which is important to the social design of computerized workplaces. Much of what has been written about social design tends to be normative in nature. The control of work comes primarily from analytical studies. Lacking normative guidelines in the area of control, writers on social design frequently — and unfortunately — ignore the entire issue. In this section that analytical studies of control and coordination in the workplace may be used to provide behavioral grounding for ideas about social design.

The importance of such a behavioral ground in forming design choices can be illustrated by analogy with architecture. From the 1930s to the 1950s, many large-scale public housing projects were constructed as high rise apartments in a sea of asphalt. The architects of these projects seem to have paid little attention to the social behavior of people who would inhabit their buildings (or, in computer system terms, their "users"). They seem to have conceptualized the boundaries of a project as encompassing only the structure and its sculptural properties, a view which is analogous to a Closed Rational systems model. Some of the larger public housing projects became squalid housing, with defaced or graffiti laden walls, and unsafe for many residents. One large housing project, Pruitt-Igoe in St. Louis, was designed in the mid-1950s and dynamited in 1972 by the agency which had built it. A film of the event showing a row of high rise buildings crumbling after the blasts is much more dramatic than most scenes of failed computer systems which go quietly unused. But the similarity is that artifacts of many kinds may not function well when their (implicit or explicit) social designs do not foster workable social systems.

Electronic Support For Mangerial Control of the Workplace

Analysts who fear that managers will use computer systems to tighten control over workers have focussed on the issue of electronic monitoring. Defenders of electronic monitoring argue that managers have a right to know how effectively their subordinates are working, and whether they are slacking off. When computerized work is relatively private and reflected in shifting screens rather than lines of people or stacks of paper, managers need new ways to learn how their subordinates are working. Critics of electronic monitoring argue that it is oppressive, unobtrusive and pervasive. The manager who walks around to see how her staff are working can talk with them about the nature of the work, the organization, and their personal lives. They can build solidarity in their work groups, although much depends upon their abilities to develop rapport and communicate. In contrast, the supervisor who stays at a distance from her subordinates and has frequent measures of activities such as keystrokes, transactions or phone calls can create a pervasive judgmental presence. They have fewer occasions to build workgroup solidarity and motivate through commitment rather than fear.

In "Big Brother and the Sweatshop" Paul Attewell examines five theoretical approaches to help understand the typical uses of computerized workplace monitoring. He notes variations in the way that business firms and public agencies organize work and technology. Attewell examines the differing predictions which one would make by using five different theoretical approaches: corporate culture, neo-Marxism, product lifecycle, contingency theory, and industrial sociology. He argues that managers have tremendous incentives in principle to learn about and control the work of their subordinates. But he observes that many practical conditions weigh against their using computer systems as instruments of surveillance in the vast majority of workplaces. Attewell's article is specially important because of the care with which he examines a variety of supervisory strategies and how managers work with and without computerized monitoring systems. He notes that managers are concerned with controlling many resources, not just labor. For example, it's likely that the manager of a work group that manages multi-million dollar investments will pay more attention to the quality of decisions being made rather than a few thousand dollars in salary costs. In contrast, the manager of a work group where labor is the most costly resource and where judgmental errors are unlikely to be catastrophic may be very anxious to shave a few thousand dollars off of the payroll by having people work to their maximum. Attewell develops an alternative model Open Systems model that integrates elements of the organizations' environment, culture, business strategy, work organization and labor market conditions.

While Attewell asks about the conditions under which organizations will monitor the activities of their staffs, Grant and Higgens ask about the effectiveness and repercussions of monitoring service workers, such as those who audit insurance claims. They developed a rich, multidimensional concept of monitoring which includes features such as the granularity of data, the range of data collected, and the variety of people who routinely see data about a person's work.

They found that many people did not object to computerized monitoring. But they also found that monitoring does not always improve performance and the quality of service. In fact, service seemed to degrade most when many aspects of performance were monitored and made available to supervisors. Grant and Higgens view monitoring as a legitimate but subtle form of managerial intervention — in terms, a social design — which can often backfire when system designers and managers do not pay close attention to people's indirect responses to monitoring.

Patterns of Professional Control

Issues of control and cooperation are not limited to workplaces that where blue collar production workers or clerks are predominant. It may be easier to conceptualize a technical or professional work group as primarily cooperative. But some analysts, like Pelle Ehn, have argued that all work is fundamentally cooperative. Kling criticized this position and noted:

Most workplaces are much less coercive than chain gangs. But the primary alternatives are not simply limitless cooperation, as if these are all-or-nothing characteristics of group relations. As Grudin points out in the case of group calendars, most professionals are not so eager to cater to their managers' preferences that they will continually inconvenience themselves and lower their productivity in order to help their manager's secretary schedule meetings. They are somewhat cooperative, but also somewhat autonomous and self-oriented. Further, some kinds of conflict in groups is critical for identifying alternative lines of action and avoiding groupthink, as long as conflicts are resolved constructively and with dignity. In practice, many working relationships can be multivalent, mix elements of cooperation, conflict, conviviality, competition, collaboration, commitment, caution, control, coercion, coordination and combat (just to stay with some "c-words"). They also involve attention to substantive tasks, managing the organization of work, genuine sociability, and even play.

It is also possible to conceptualize even a technical or professional workplace as subject to rigorous and increasing managerial control. Perrolle examines how managers can use expert systems and other advanced computer technologies to reduce the skill levels of professional jobs. Perrolle draws on Harry Braverman's argument that owners and managers relentlessly try to enhance their control over workers to reduce labor costs. One major managerial strategy is reducing the skills required for most jobs, thus enabling them to hire less expensive workers. Perrolle illustrates this theme through the example of computerized "application generators". Some of these facilities simplify the production of computer programs so they can be written by clerical workers paid $20,000 per year, rather than by university-trained programmers paid $40,000 per year. Perrolle argues that expert systems may also be applied toward reducing the skill levels required for professional jobs. As skill levels of jobs are reduced, so is their pay, autonomy, status, and perhaps their intrinsic interest.

Perrolle's argument ignores fundamental aspects of the computerized professional workplace. Spreadsheets, like Lotus 1-2-3 and Microsoft's Excel, are the primary software types that fueled the market for PCs in businesses in the mid-1980s. While it is possible to regiment and de-skill jobs with spreadsheets, the majority of applications are geared towards professionals and/or their clerical assistants. It is likely that professionals and managers, rather than clerical workers, will be the major users of any new information systems, absorbing these innovations at a higher rate than local programmers can devise them. Organizations and work groups frequently standardize their software; word processors, databases, and spreadsheets. This does not, however, automatically regiment the overall character of work.

In a rich and provocative field study, Wanda Orlikowski examines how a large international computer-consulting firm used Computer Assisted Software Engineering (CASE) tools to reorganize work. Unlike other cases in which social design was implicit, this firm has adopted a very explicit social design — but one which is still based on a Rational Systems view of the workplace. They hire college graduates and MBAs with no significant professional computing experience and trains them with their own methods. It reviews the newer consultants with tough "up or out" hurdles every two years. Orlikowski's account of this firm's use of customized CASE tools has some important parallels with Perrolle's characterization of intellectual assembly lines. The CASE tools were designed to enforce a specific sequence of design activities, for example by requiring that data tables be fully defined before they are used in a program.

The firm spent less effort in training newer recruits than they spent on similar employees in previous years. She reports that the younger consultants did not realize that their jobs required less skill for them than for consultants who had worked without the CASE tools. In fact, they liked the windowed CASE tools with easy-to-use menus and the ability to easily edit changes without rewriting whole documents. Some of the intermediate level consultants had found key ways to work around some of the CASE tools' restrictions when they were working in a time crunch, but managers frowned on these workarounds.

Kling and Iacono take a different approach to workplace monitoring and the control of work. Their empirical study — based on Open Natural System assumptions — examines the ways in which computerization alters social control and coordination in workplaces. Most analysts who examine the use of computer-based systems to tighten social control rely upon some conceptual model of managerial authority. Kling and Iacono introduce an "institutional model of social control" in which information can flow in any direction (up, down, and laterally) and in which people in different organizational units can try to enforce norms upon people in other organizational units.

Kling and Iacono observe complex patterns of negotiation and control that go beyond the traditional hierarchy. They rigorously compare the explanatory power of the institutional model with two other models, hierarchical managerial authority and negotiated order (which focusses upon lateral peer realtionships). The institutional model of social control is important because it shows that social behavior can be controlled through information flows and people that extend beyond the immediate behavior setting in which workers use computer-based information systems.

Further, they showed that a workers' peers, or even people who are lower in the hierarchy, can use certain kinds of operational inofrmation systems to control other's behavior. Kling and Iacono focussed their study on complex inventory control systems in manufacturing firms. But their points pertain to groupware or any other computerized system where peers can see each other's work performance through the system. Their study suggests the type of research that may be appropriate — but has yet to be done — leading toward a different portrait of organizational control patterns and different ideas about the social design of work.

The Integration of Computing into Work

The vast majority of articles and books about computerization and work are written as if computer systems are highly reliable and graceful instruments. From a Rational Systems perspective, integration of these systems into the work place is relatively unproblematic; the few issues that might arise are solvable by purely technical means (e.g., converting files from one format to another, installing compatible communications processors, etc.). There are relatively few published studies of the ways that people actually use software systems in their work — which features do they use, how do they meet and resolve problems caused by systems or gaps in their own skills and how does the use of computerized systems alter the coherence and complexity of work? From a Natural Systems perspective, systems — including the people who use them and the work places in which they are used — are much more dynamic at all levels. Integration therefore becomes a much more complex issue — one which is not resolved at installation time, but continues throughout the life of the system. Whether or not system designers face this issue, the people who use the systems will face it; their work life depends to a large degree on the gracefulness (or non-gracefulness) of the ongoing integration process.

ANOMALIES

In "The Integration of Computing and Routine Work," Les Gasser studied anomalies common in the daily use of computing systems. Anomalies are discrepancies between a person's expectation of behavior and the actuality. Anomalies include system bugs, but they go much further. For example, in 1990 the State of Massachusetts billed the city of Princeton, MA one cent in interest after it paid a bill for a ten cent underpayment of taxes.

Each of these transactions cost a postage stamp, as well as several dollars in staff time and computing resources. The Wall Street Journal reporter viewed the situation as anomalous because one would not expect organizations to routinely invest many dollars in attempting to collect a few cents. However, the computer program was probably working as it was designed — to compute interest on all underpayments and produce accurate bills for interest due to the State of Massachusetts.

Gasser views computer use as a social act rather than as an individual act. He discusses computerized information systems that are developed, used, maintained, and repaired, by teams of people — people who relay their beliefs about system values, uses, limits, and problems to their co-workers. In addition, the people in Gasser's study depend upon other groups in their organization for key resources such as data, training, and equipment fixes. Anomalies occur due to the interactions between these groups, which are not organized like firemen to race to each other's aid at a moment's notice.

Gasser argues that discrepancies are widespread. The anomalies of computing may be reduced by improved equipment, but they cannot be eliminated. Gasser's argument sheds some light on the question of why computerization may not enhance productivity as readily as many analysts expect. It gives us insight as to why certain jobs become more complex with computerization — since men and women who use computers sometimes need to account for these differences and work around them.

Users of network systems, too, may encounter anomalies. Some writers compare these systems in terms of features, ease of use, and similar criteria. But system-comparison articles seem to assume that each organization will choose only one system to implement, that each user will learn and use that system and that system only, that the chosen hardware/software package will support all possible connectivity requirements of all users in the organization, and that the system will remain unchanged for long periods of time except for periodic "improvements" and added efficiency-producing features. But some organizations may use multiple and dynamically-evolving network systems.

In a system such as this, it is not surprising to find incompatibilities and features that are far from "user friendly". Multiple software packages require us to remember at least 14 different keystroke combinations even for the "simple" task of exiting a program. Electronic mail addressing schemes differ widely between the systems; for example, we are easily able to find the address for any user of the Academic Computing mainframe but are often unable to locate people who use the Graduate School of Management (GSM) system. At GSM, it is easy to attach documents in a variety of formats to any electronic mail message.

Unfortunately, these attachments cannot be easily read correctly when the message goes outside the local network. The authors regularly transmit documents from one home to the other through the intermediary of PC-to-mainframe file transfer; these documents can even retain the imbedded formatting information of common PC-based word processor.

Time Saving and Time Consumption

Networks and electronic communications can intensify these problems. In most accounts of electronic communications, basic on-demand connectivity from the user's terminal or computer to a network is simply assumed to be present. But even this minimum requirement may not always be guaranteed or timely. Both authors, when they are working from home, dial into a network system through ordinary telephone lines.

In one case, this telephone line is shared with the rest of the family, which means that occasional waiting for access is inevitable. Even the other author's dedicated "computer-phone" line fails to solve the problem of a busy-signal at the other end; university networks are notoriously sensitive to semester-end overload as students — who also have access from their home computers — rush to complete assignments simultaneously. In the worst case, telephone lines may fail entirely, preventing all network use for an extended period of time; this actually happened to both authors during a series of winter storms. Once the delays have been overcome and connectivity has been established, other time-consumers come into the foreground: time-consumers associated with each of the major models of network communications.

Some people may rely upon electronic-mail to communicate with others. Many groups provide a "distribution list" which makes it easy to send a single message simultaneously to a particular group of people. This capability is often mentioned as one of the key advantages of electronic mail. Distribution lists are used at many sites that have been studied by academic researchers. But since many messages apply to only some people who subscribe to any specific distribution list, many subscribers may receive a large number of messages that they see as irrlevent to them. One of the few complaints reported in Hiltz' survey focused on "group messages that are voluminous, unnecessary, or of little general interest." Regular electronic mail users expect to perform some amount of routine maintenance work in sorting, filing, cataloging, and retrieving these messages. Only some email systems provide easy-to-use software tools to support these activities.

The unfortunate person who, by choice or necessity, participates in many distribution lists can easily have his or her electronic "inbox" filled each day to unmanageable levels. Tom Finholt, an active researcher in the electronic communications area, reported to the authors the case of a person working in one of his research sites, who belonged to 450 electronic mail distribution lists. Even at much less dramatic levels, the quantity of messages — from both distribution lists and individual correspondence — can be problematic. One author's inbox varies from 15 to 50 messages each workday. But when he travels, he is sometimes unable to connect with his home system. This can cause an accumulation of perhaps 300 to 400 messages, which may take from 5 to 8 hours to work through after his return home — which in turn causes understandable family resentment at the additional "lost" time.

An alternative to distribution lists is communication via electronic bulletin boards, in which messages are posted by individuals but are publicly available for reading by anyone who uses the network. Among the most popular bulletin board systems are those of the Internet, which is a system that is widely available both to universities and to private research organizations. These bulletin boards are organized hierarchically by topic, with major headings such as "comp" for computing, "rec" for recreation, and so on. Some of the boards are accessible to anyone for direct posting of messages; some are moderated (that is, messages are sent first to a person who serves as moderator, who then sorts, edits, and posts blocks of messages for reading). The total of board topics on the Internet now numbers nearly 2000 — many more than any one person is likely to even casually scan. Some of these topics attract only a few messages per day, or per week. But others can vary up to hundreds of messages per day, for example political themes during the presidential campaign or Gulf War-related topics during that crisis. To the reader, this quantity of messages can be overwhelming.

Another major function of electronic communications is to locate and transfer information among the many sites on a network. Measured by sheer volume of data transmitted, this is major use of the Internet — and it is growing in relation to other services such as mail and newsgroups. New Internet facilities which searching for files and transferring them, such as gopher and World Wide Web, have become very popular. From a Rational Systems perspective, virtually instant access to thousands of data files which are maintained on hundreds of computers worldwide offers inescapable efficiencies for "knowledge workers" such as researchers and journalists. This advantage may be realized in some cases. But even the most efficiency-minded information-searcher may take many false turns through multiple levels of access menus, and may spend a great deal of time browsing through information of peripheral value at best. Some commercial "value-added" networks (for example, Compuserve) seem to be designed to encourage their clients to spend as much (chargeable) time as possible doing just that: browsing through mountains of information, whether or not it is of central value.

Infrastructure for Supporting Computer Use

Workable computing arrangements depend upon a set of supporting physical, technological or social resources. Physical resources include space for equipment.

Technological resources can require electricity and communication lines. Social resources may be comprised of people skilled in the use and repair of equipment as well as the practices for allocating resources. These collective resources are termed the computing infrastructure by Kling and his colleagues.

The social infrastructure for supporting people's use of computing is a key element in any computerization effort People report having better quality worklives in workgroups where the computing infrastructure for supporting training and consulting is best developed. Further, financially poorer organizations, like many public schools, sometimes have trouble effectively using gifts of advanced computer systems because of weakness in their computing infrastructure, especially limited technical support. Training is one element of computing infrastructure that receives continuing professional attention. But computing infrastructure refers to a much richer array of resources and practices and is a central element of web models of computing.

It is common for images of simplification to dominate talk about computerization, regardless of the complexity of systems. Clement reports a case of computerization for secretaries in which managers characterized new systems as "super typewriters" that did not require special training. They were very much mistaken.

Many of the popular "full featured" PC software packages for text processing, spreadsheets, and databases include hundreds of features. Narratives that focus on the capabilities of systems usually suggest that people can readily have all the advantages that the features offer. Actual behavior often differs from these expectations.

The majority of people who use these powerful programs learn only a small fraction of the available capabilities — enough to do their most immediate work. Moreover, it is increasingly common for many workers to use multiple computer systems, often with conflicting conventions, further complicating people's ability to "use computer systems to their fullest advantage." This dilemma can be partially resolved through the adoption of comparatively uncomplicated systems.

Providing staff training and having available consultants can increase the practicality of the system. But organizations that try to keep "overhead costs" low often seem more willing to buy new computer systems than to invest in internal training and consulting. Managers often decide that supporting computer use with training and consulting is too expensive. Training is not cheap; an organization may pay $500 in labor time for a professional to learn to use a package that costs $150 to purchase.

One of the authors vividly remembers a research administrator of a major food processing firm who was using a popular and powerful spreadsheet for budget projects. He wanted to print out reports in different fonts, such as printing budget categories in larger bolder print. But he did not know how to do this. He believed that "it could be done easily" because he saw such a report in an advertisement. And, most important, he treated his ignorance as a personal failing. However, he would have had to learn his spreadsheet's macro facility to print in varied fonts. His manual provided no clues about the techniques for changing fonts within a report. In some organizations he might have turned to an information center with skilled consultants.

In this company, the PC consultants were overworked installing new PCs and had no time to train the men or women who use them or consult with them on software use. This was not a critical problem for the manager. But it indicates how many organizations expect white collar workers to learn to effectively use computer systems on their own, with little support besides limited manuals and advice from co-workers. Windowing systems are another complex family of environments whose actual use has many nuances. They are sold as easy to use., while they actually daunt non-specialists who try to configure them without expert help. Computer systems do not work perfectly, further adding to the skills people need to develop and complicating their work.

Christine Bullen and John Bennett examined how people actually integrate computer systems to support collaborative work in groups (groupware) into their work. They report how several work groups attempted to use some of today's best commercially available groupware systems with mixed results. Their informants found the value of the electronic mail features of these systems to be significant, despite the fact that a number of the electronic mail features were not used to full advantage. Others found many of the offered features hard to use, or not worth the effort.

Notably, Bullen and Bennett discovered that many groups eventually reorganized their work to take the best advantage of their groupware. For example, the usage of electronic calendars to schedule meetings requires that all participants keep detailed calendars up to date on the computer system, even if they spend much of their time out of the office. Many managers and professionals hope that they can computerize effectively by installing appropriate equipment, rather than by reorganizing work when they (re)computerize. Bullen and Bennett make a provocative attempt to characterize high performing groups and found that they are not always the most computerized. They argue that group members and their managers have worked hard to create work environments that have "clear elevating goals," and which support and reward commitment. These groups have developed effective social systems with coherent goals and related rewards as well as adopting technologies that might help improve their performance.

There is considerable unpublished controversy about this kind of analysis, since many technologists and computer vendors try to convince computer using organizations that appropriate new technologies alone will improve working styles and organizational effectiveness. During the 1990s interesting technologies such as expert systems, groupware and graphical interfaces will be written about by technologists and journalists as if they can significantly improve the ways that people work without requiring important changes in the way groups organize their work. Careful studies of work with new computing technologies, like Bullen and Bennett's study, suggest that new technologies alone are unlikely to be magic potions that can automatically improve work just by appearing in a workplace.

In this chapter, examined several ways in which researchers and practitioners can advance their understanding of computerized and networked work life. First, examined the social design of computer and communications systems to help indicate how technologies are shaped by organizations as part of a computerization effort. The consequences of computing or networking for work organization and workers are byproducts of socio-technical configurations, or social designs, rather than of technology alone.

Scholars and professionals who examine the usability and consequences of computerized systems rely upon specific conceptions of new information technologies and heir relationships to organizational changes. This section also examined four common conceptual models of organizational behavior which inform these analyses: combinations of Rational and Natural, and Open and Closed systems.

Second, we have conceptually integrated the analysis of work places that employ more "traditional" computing arrangements (i.e., central computing facilities or stand-alone PCs) and those that use computerized networks and communication systems. Most empirical studies of work with networks tend to focus on actions of the communicants, without examining the broader ecology of the organizational settings in which the systems function, and in which people who do not directly use the networks may control key resources for acquiring, regulating, and supporting system use.

Third, we have located the study of computerization and work life within an explicit set of models drawn from sociological theories of organization. The connection between the two topics is an important one. Organizational theory, by itself, rarely examines the dynamics of work.

Studies of work life, on the other hand, seldom study the dynamics of organizations in which the work is done. A few studies link these "macro" and "micro" views of behavior in organizations, but the two levels of analysis should be combined in much more synergistic ways in future research.

We have focused on the tacit conceptions of organizational behavior that permeate much of the literature on computing and work life. Analyses which rely on Closed Rational systems assumptions dominate the professional literature and are common in the scholarly literature. Closed Rational systems models are relatively simple and easiest to write about and comprehend. As each new technology enters the marketplace, its advocates tend to write about its virtues in ways that presume that organizations act as Rational systems, and usually as Closed Rational systems.

Closed Rational systems models can be unduly narrow, and even misleading. They often exclude important conditions that affect the roles of computer systems and their users. For example, they assume that all organizations adopt particular computer systems because of their value for expediting certain tasks. They ignore the possibility that some participants convince upper managers to adopt computer technologies because of other considerations, such as image, helping to attract highly qualified technical staff, etc. For practitioners, Closed Rational systems models are troublesome because they are likely to underestimate the complexity of implementing and using computers and networks. And they emphasize only a limited range of values on which to base computer system design decisions.

We have found that the Open Systems models, both rational and natural, help us to understand the incentives that people have for using computing and network systems, in ways that are much more "true-to-life" than the Closed System models. Many issues of coordination in work lead people to interact with others outside of their immediate organizational unit. Consequently studies of coordination, work and computerization should rest on Open Systems models. Further, the Open Natural System models also provide important explanations for many of the opportunities and problems that are encountered in systems implementation and use, and can help us to better predict the actual value of these systems.

To summarize the comparative explanatory power of the four families of models. An analyst using Closed Rational Systems models of organizational behavior would examine telecommuting in terms of the tasks, social relationships, and efficiencies within the work group. But this perspective would have trouble accounting for social relationships between work group members and those outside of their organization. Rational Open Systems models could include relationships between employees working at dispersed geographic locations — including in the home — and people in other organizations with whom they work. But we would still focus only on their work tasks.

We would ignore other important social relationships that make homes into distinctive kinds of work places, not simply remote spaces that are free of distractions. By moving to an Open Natural view, we are able to assess the interactions between the employee, the work tasks, and all of the social actors and their demands — such as children, neighbors, and other family members — that make up the social ecology of the telecommuter.

The Open Natural systems models provide a sounder conceptual foundation for understanding diverse forms of work with computing and networks. They also assist us in identifying appropriate boundaries for the social design of systems. In designing a telecommuting work system, for example, these boundaries should include the non-task- oriented social actors as well as the computing equipment and network software.

Conceptions of organizations which rest on Rational systems models predominate in technological communities. However, they are not scientifically sound ways to understand the changing worlds of work as they are supported and constrained by new technologies. Organizational theorists moved beyond Rational systems models by the 1930s. It's important for those who socially design computer and networked systems to think with organizational models that are as contemporary as the technologies which they wish to understand and use!

6

Computerization and Safe Systems

Computer systems are becoming more technically complex, and development times can sometimes frustrate customers. Simple applications software, like word processors, have expanded from thousands to millions of lines of program code as vendors pack them wit h ever more sophisticated features. Powerful computer chips, which serve as central processors for Macs, PCs, and engineering work stations, contain the equivalent of millions of transistors. Product designers are adding "smart controls" to household and industrial products, from air conditioners and bread makers to medical devices, telephone switching systems, banking systems, electric power plants, as well as food and chemical processing plants through the use of software and chips. These newer technolo gies are often more convenient, flexible and reliable than their predecessors.

However, it is common for those who rely on computers or computer based services to experience various kind of malfunctions, problems, and aberrant computer behavior. A word processor may hang, causing an author to lose a few brilliant paragraphs, or find that a document representing a month's work is corrupted. An auto mated teller machine can "eat a bank card" and refuse to eject it after a transaction. A new homeowner might receive a $4,000 water bill because of an ill-designed meter reading program. Or a telephone answering machine may require such a complex and rigi d sequence of commands to replay messages from another phone, that a person erases his calls when he intends to repeat them.

These agonizing events are usually treated as the "minor irritants of modern life" and are illustrated in R. Aminzade's article about computer driven "voice-mail". Michael Slavitch's article examines both the "irritant" and the "blind faith" attitude people sometimes display towards computers and their systems. Slavitch uses his personal experience as an example. A convenient automated book-not ice service from his library failed to work properly. The librarian's reaction when he complained about the malfunction graphically illustrates a more serious problem. The librarian "insisted that the 'system' must be 'reliable' and 'almost always' works ," and that he had no basis for complaining.

Both articles appeared in the electronic newsletter, *RISKS-FORUM Digest* moderated by Peter G. Neumann of SRI International, with support from the Association for Computing Machinery (ACM). *RISKS-FORUM Digest* is an important forum which gives computer specialists an opportunity to discuss unsafe computer systems designs and organizational practices. While *RISKS-FORUM Digest* includes many accounts where accidents have been avoided or where the consequences are mostly irritating, its contributors also discuss and debate the nature of life-threatening systems hazards.

In extreme cases new information technologies have increased the vulnerability of communities. For example, computer system problems have lead to millions of people losing telephone service, 85,000 airline passengers being grounded for hours, people bein g killed by medical equipment, as well as people and organizations losing billions of dollars. Between the individual hassles and problems that injure millions are the thousands of system snafus involving computers that don't appear in the news or profes sional literature because they harm or inconvenience only people who work within a specific organization.

While many computer systems are occasionally unreliable, their errors and failures, like Aminzade's voice mail example, usually do little harm. What is critical are computers and systems that are **unsafe** — and render groups vulnerable by inadverten tly leading to human injury or significant financial losses. When reviewing system safety and social vulnerability, consider the wide range of computer-based systems whose reliable function is indispensable for human health, and well being. These includ e transportation (air, rail, automobile, ship), national defense, communication, financial exchanges, payrolls, medicine, law-enforcement, nuclear power, elections, elevators, chemical plants, space exploration, mining, the food industry, and record-keeping associated with many social and governmental services.

Computer Science professor Nancy Leveson makes the key point that system safety should be defined in terms of hazards rather than accidents or disasters. She notes that "System-safety engineers define safety in terms of hazards and risk. A hazard is a set of conditions (i.e., a state) that can lead to an accident given certain environmental conditions."

Hazards can include guard gates not lowering when trains approach traffic crossings, a warning light burning out in an electric power plant, a comp uter system deleting a file without asking for an operator's confirmation, or a company's failure to perform scheduled maintenance on key equipment. These hazards increase the likelihood of accidents — events that result in loss or injury — occurring. B ut, as Leveson and other safety analysts note, accidents are often caused (or avoided) because of multiple factors. For example, a guard gate may not lower when a train crosses a road, but the drivers may all spot the engine's headlight or hear its whistl e and stay off the tracks.

In many cases, hazards lead to "near misses" (or incidents) — potential accidents that were avoided. Near-miss incidents occur, according to various estimates, from 10 to over 100 times more frequently than actual accidents. In special case s of systems and services where many lives or huge amounts of money are at risk, organizations institute procedures to report, track, and investigate incidents, not just accidents.

For example, the U.S. Federal Aviation Administration requires pilots and air traffic controllers to report a variety of incidents, such as planes flying too close to each other. However, such few companies create incident reports about their operations and those that do tend to treat them as highly confidential, internal inf ormation. The public usually learns about system and service hazards through reports of accidents.

On June 26, 1991, over six million Bell Atlantic telephones were cut off for seven hours in Washington, DC, Maryland, Virginia and West Virginia. Problems with Pacific Bell's network equipment in Los Angeles and Orange County, California, affected three million lines for about two-and-a-half hours on the same day. This loss of nine million phones in one day was one of the largest phone network failures in U.S. history.

The problem was traced to a switching center in Baltimore, Maryland where a faulty circuit board triggered new switching software to pump erroneous messages into the phone system. But beyond these technical glitches were other potential organizational hazards. The equipment vendor, DSC, was aware of similar problems that had briefly shut down millions of telephones in California on June 10. But it appears that DSC never informed the telephone companies about the nature of the equipment faults.

In addition, regulatory arrangements prevented the regional phon e companies from working closely together to improve the reliability of service (Mason, 1991a). The published accounts of this massive failure were sketchy, but it appears that communication gaps between DSC and the regional phone companies may have been as important as the specific failed circuit board in triggering this disaster. It is common for organizations and journalists to identify some equipment component or some individual operator as the cause of major mishaps (Perrow, 1984). But often the caus es are more complex and interwoven.

Breakdowns in systems that we take for granted and think of as very reliable can help us learn about computer systems hazards. On 10:10 a.m. Tuesday, Sept.

17, 1991, AT&T cut over to diesel generators at a switching center in lower Manhattan, N.Y. The move, part of a power-saving agreement with Consolidated Edison Co. of New York, Inc., was requested because the summer was particularly hot and air conditioners drove up the demand for electric power. However, this move also set off a massive telephone outage that left air traffic controllers in the Northeast "on hold" and 85,000 air passengers on the ground.

During or soon after the cut to internal power, rectifiers in the center's power supply failed. The rectifiers convert AC power to DC. An AT&T protective meter-relay which was improperly set triggered at 52.8 volts instead of at 53.5 volts. The failure of the meter-relay in the rectifiers initiated a series of other failures and mistakes . When the normal electric power failed, the system immediately switched to back-up batteries. Technicians monitoring the network failed to read several alarms properly, and did not conduct inspections that would have allowed them to discover the problem earl ier. When AT&T technicians attempted to routinely convert back to commercial power at about 4:30 pm., they discovered the failed rectifiers, which prevented them from using normal electrical power. By then the batteries, which have about a six-hour life span, were close to drained.

Twenty minutes later, they gave out for good. Faulty maintenance and poor judgement further compounded the original problem. In one location, an alarm light did not work because its bulb was burned out; and in another place, an audible alarm did not sound because one of its wires had been cut; and elsewhere a standard-procedure maintenance walk through was not done as it should have been. While power was restored by ea rly evening, the airports did not clear till midnight. Because the telephones were inoperative, few passengers were able to call and inform others about the delayed flights. Ironically, travellers with cellular phones were able to phone their friends. And there are apocryphal stories of stranded passengers passing cellular telephones around inside grounded aircraft so other passengers could use them.

While a computer system was not implicated in this telephone systems failure, it illustrates some of the ways in which major accidents occur through the *interaction* of several social and technical systems (power systems, phone systems, and air tra ffic control systems, in this case). They can involve a mixture of component failures, confusion by operators about what the nature and scope of problems really are, and by gaps in organizational routines (such as maintaining various equipment). Sociologist Charles Perrow discovered similar complexities when he investigated the causes of the nuclear plant that nearly had a meltdown — Three Mile Island, near Harrisburg, Pennsylvania. Perrow found that many industrial accidents involve an interacting mixture of technical and organizational causes. Perrow coined the catchy term "normal accident" (or "systems accident") to refer to damage that occurs because of multiple interacting causes. Perrow raises provocative questions abo ut the ways in which some systems that combine technologies and organizational practices (including staff training, preventive maintenance) are designed so that periodic accidents should be expected.

"Safety-Critical Computing" Jonathan Jacky, a scientist who develops software for a radiation therapy clinic, focusses upon a similarly complex, but more fatal, set of events. He begins with the story how a new highly computerized r adiation machine designed to treat cancer was sometimes overdosing patients to the extent that some died or were maimed. This is a remarkable set of mishaps, because the Therac-25 was heralded as a "better cure." Further, the Therac-25 seemed to be effectively giving radiation therapy to thousands of people suffering from cancer.

Jacky shows us how these deaths and maimings were the byproducts of flawed technical system designs, hospital practices, the vendor's behavior, and the weak system fo r regulating computerized medical equipment. The Therac-25 killed and maimed people not simply because of technical failures, but because of complementary failures in the organizational systems that supported its daily use. He then discusses how computerized control systems embedded in airplanes, trains, and other equipment where mishaps can kill, can be subject to some of these same organizational failures. Jacky also considers several possible solutions, including licensing software engineers for safety -critical systems, and tightening the procedures for certifying the safety of medical devices and other major systems.

In "Aging Airways" Gary Stix examines the daunting obstacles that impede the U.S. Federal Aviation Administration (FAA) efforts to modernize the air traffic control system (ATC). Stix recounts a fascinating story in which the current ATC system depends on 25 year old Unisys computers, and archaic procedures in which air traffic controllers scribble flight information on tiny paper strips. The air traffic control system is remarkably reliable, due largely to the controllers' skill and moral commitment to a irline safety. While IBM won a contract to modernize the ATC system, the price tag has almost doubled to about $31,000,000,000 and the project is four years overdue. Gary Stix describes some of the complexities of one apparently simple change: computerizing and eliminating the paper strips in ways that don't reduce the controllers' ability to monitor aircraft. Even though information and computer professionals view paper as worse than digital media, IBM's digital designs were much clumsier and compromise d air safety much more than simple paper strips.

STRATEGIES FOR IMPROVING SYSTEMS SAFETY

Despite the many difficulties catalogued so far, it is apparent from existing systems (space exploration, airline transportation, etc.) that safe systems are not always an impossible dream. In fact, we take such safety so much for granted, that the fat al explosion of the space-shuttle Challenger in January 1986 shocked the nation and cost NASA immense credibility. While the technical failure of the Challenger was caused by faulty seals (o-rings), the problem was known to certain manager s and engineers in the firm (Morton-Thiokol) that designed the rockets. The nature of a managerial decision to risk the shuttle's launching and cover-up the engineering criticisms of possible o-ring failures was widely reported after a Congressional inquiry into this disaster. Heimann published an interesting analysis which shows how a change in NASA's organizational structure also made this kind of disaster more likely.

There is a strong cultural bias in North America to focus on discrete causes for system failures — like a broken device, a software bug, a single person's error, or even a coverup. We are much less likely to examine whether the ways that organizations ar e structured or the character of their cultures can lead to system failures. Scholars are systematically studying organizational failures and high performance organizations to better understand these issues. Onl y recently have systematic organizational-level analyses influenced the information and computer science professions. But professional interest in developing safe systems should help fuel broader interest in systematic organizational analysis.

There have been sustained studies of technological strategies for improving the quality of software designs. Software engineering methods incorporate various error-reducing strategies, including systematic testing strategies. The licensing of professiona l programmers, has been suggested. And computer scientists have worked hard to develop a meaningful theoretical basis for software design.

Formal verification techniques may help uncover the discrepancies between a program's specification and the actual program. For example, in the fall 1994, Intel admitted that its highly touted and widely sold Pentium chip was not 100% reliable in carryin g out arithmetic calculations. Intel admitted the flaws only after a mathematician publicly criticized the chip's accuracy. Further, Intel lost credibility when it minimized the importance of the problem and was unwilling to automatically replace the mill ions of Pentium chips that it had sold. Intel's spokesmen claimed that the computational errors were exceptionally rare and would show up only in specially complex calculations. Critics retorted that the errors could occur more frequently and that even c ommon financial calculations, could lead to erroneous results. Formally verifying the correctness of the chip's mathematical routines might have avoided the Pentium's problems.

The Pentium fiasco may lead more chip vendors to try verifying the correctness of their chips. Even so, vendors' claims should be carefully scrutinized, especially claims of "software engineering" and "program verification", and particularly in contexts w here mistakes may be irreversible and catastrophic. Discussions of program verification tend to flounder due to confusion over what the "verification" process actually involves. The Verifiable Integrated Processor for Enhanced Reliability (VIPER) micropr ocessor was designed in the late 1980s for safety critical military, space, and transportation applications, such as "fly-by wire" aircraft and railroad crossing controllers. VIPER includes the equivalent of several million transistors. The sheer complexity of these chips makes guarantees of correctness very alluring. VIPER's designers used mathematical proof techniques to help ensure absolute correctness and freedom from design errors. But it was the subject of exaggerated advertising after it was "proven to be free" of design errors. For example, the proofs of correctness do not insure that th e original specifications were correct, and analysts subsequently claimed to have found four specification errors in VIPER's design.

Some of the debates on the meaning and significance of formal verification have been very heated. Brian Smith's paper relative consistency between a program specification and program code. Smith goes on to observe, however, that if the specification itself reflects a world model that is deficient in some relevant respect, the deficiency will carry over to the prog ram, thus remaining undetected by any formal consistency proof. This point is crucial, for it implies that a computer system with perfectly functioning hardware, and software that adheres accurately to a set of written requirements, may still result in s erious failures. The indispensability of robust testing should be apparent in the face of this argument. Still, software engineers will argue that formal methods help improve programs by encouraging people to carefully consider their designs and develop simpler systems which are easier to verify. Jon Jacky, for example, comments,

> ...it can be very valuable, and it provides far more assurance than we get from most projects. Even being in a position to attempt such a verification requires that somebody provide a complete and explicit specification that documents what t he system is expected to do and reveals the builders' assumptions about what the system will demand of its environment. Most projects never produce such a specification, and as a result the expected system behaviors and the assumptions about the environm ent cannot be reviewed or criticized or even examined because they are hidden in the program text itself — usually encoded in some obscure way (they don't call it code for nothing). Because of this, the specification can be as valuable as the verificat ion itself — maybe moreso.

Safe technological designs are a key element of safe systems. Jacky's article illustrates how the behavior of equipment users, such as radiological technicians in the case of the Therac-25, is also crucial. The 1991 fiasco in which a power system failure in one of AT&T's switching centers grounded air lanes at three major airports illustrates how high quality preventive maintenance can also play a key role. Safe systems are most likely to be operated by high performance organizations, that place a premium on the safety of their customers, clients, and employees. Gary Stix's account of the way that the FAA is able to operate a highly reliable air traffic control system with ancient and unreliable technologies underlines this point. However, relatively few organizations have the safety consciousness of the FAA. Given the infusion of computer technology into everyday affairs, it is only to be expected that malfunctions will result in inconvenience, serious harm, or even threats to life, in an ever-widening s pectrum.

WHEN ARE COMPUTERS SAFE FOR PEOPLE WHO USE THEM?

That computer use can be a cause of health problems is a relatively new concept. If people are asked to associate the terms "computers" and "health" they are likely to imagine applications like expert systems applied to medical diagnosis or perhaps health insurance record systems. However, long-term intensive computer users may be susceptible to a significant set of ailments, including headaches, visual ailments (ie., blurred vision, double vision, color fringes, deterioration of visual acuity) and painf ul muscular strains that — in extreme cases, can make it hard for a person to cut a slice of bread with a knife. Workers' compensation claims related to repetitive strain injuries (RSI) are skyrocketing, and many lawsuits against employers are pending. "Caught in the Grip of RSI," Evan Williamson gives us a first-hand account of his predicament that includes these revelations:.

" About three-quarters of the way through the project, I noticed an odd, tired feeling spreading over the backs of my hands and up my forearms. Thinking it was simple fatigue, I promised myself a long break from the computer when the projec t was done, readjusted my hands to a more comfortable position, and continued my work.... Over the next couple of months, I started to feel what could best be described as electric shocks running up my forearms. These were rare at first, but became com mon throughout the workday. What finally sent me to the doctor was a large, painful lump beneath my skin at the intersection of the base of my right thumb and wrist."

Williamson describes how his supervisor seemed more concerned with getting him to work harder than with minimizing his suffering. And some doctors and lawyers don't believe that RSI is a valid cause for complaint. For example, hand surgeon Morton L. Kasd an, M.D., a Fellow of the American College of Occupational and Environmental Medicine (ACOEM) and chairman of its Committee on Ergonomics, don't endorse complaints like Williamson's:

"Life without pain does not exist, period. Jobs without pain do not exist. Often, the psychosocial factors are more critical to the incidence of CTDs (cumulative trauma disorders) .... If you look at people with chronic pain syndrome, more t han 80 percent of them had some kind of psychological problem while growing up. With many of these CTD patients, if you talk to their employers, you'll find they're not model employees, they're not good workers, and there's usually a precipitating even t to that medical claim, such as a reprimand, or they're about to lose their job. There's more here than a job or a computer or a chair: there are a lot of other factors that need to be looked at."

The editors of *Managing Office Technology* (1993) report the way that a British court ruled against a financial reporter who claimed that he had severe pain and lost wages after he developed RSI five years earlier. The British judge ruled that the c oncept of RSI is "meaningless" and had "no place in the medical books". Despite the skepticism over RSI, it is easy to find ergonomic aids such as wrist rests and more hand-friendly keyboards for sale in many computer stores. In fact, some computer manu facturers are placing warning labels on keyboards, if for no reason other than to protect themselves from potential lawsuits for RSI. In fact, IBM and other keyboard manufacturers have been sued for knowing that traditional computer keyboards can cause RS I and not warning computer users. According to Savage (1993:41),

Vendors find themselves faced with a dilemma. If they opt for safer designs, it implies their earlier products are unsafe. Yet, they may eventually be liable through negligence and product liability if they are found to have sold equipment tha t has harmed someone. Some vendors market safe products to companies, but do not make that information known to the general public.

"Office Automation's Threat to Health and Productivity," Omar Khalil, and Jessie Melcher discuss the rapid rise of reported RSI cases in the United States and Australia. They observe that:

Computers have turned what was once the unseen work of the office into discrete keystrokes that can be counted and sped up. Computers store and retrieve data quickly. Users can type faster while having less control over the pace of their w ork. Word processors pose special problems since they allow workers to type up to

240 characters per minute for hours without a break, and research results suggest that workers who type for more than five hours a day at a computer have 12 times as great risk of developing RSIs as those who spend less time.

People who used traditional typewriters were less at risk for RSI because they moved in more diverse ways to push the carriage of mechanical typewriters or to stop briefly and feed new sheets of paper. These simple activities required a broader range of p hysical movement from even the fastest or most highly pressured typists. And, as Khalil and Melcher note, "Office workers who once might have mixed typing with filing, answering phones, and countless other tasks may now simply sit at their computers an d type."

In the United States, a number of organizations have made serious efforts to reduce the risks of RSI. In one ironic case, the insurance firm Blue Cross had trouble finding workman's insurance for its own office workers.

In 1990 most of the 3500 employees at Blue Cross of California sat at the same-size workstations and used a desktop computer or a terminal or both. Throughout the company, graphic designers, secretaries, programmers, data entry people, insur ance underwriters, claims processors, managers, and others complained of pain in the neck, arms, hands, and shoulders. That year 26 people were unable to do their jobs due to debilitating pain and filed workers' compensation claims. These injuries cost the company a staggering $1.6 million in 1990 alone.

In response to these conditions, Blue Cross's Ellen Ignatius was authorized to purchase new ergonomic office furniture that better fit each worker. In addition

Ignatius and her staff showed Blue Cross's employees proper ways to sit and work, how to do reg ular exercises, and how often to take stretch breaks.

Other companies, such as Levi Strauss (jeans maker) and Sun Microsystems (workstation producer) ave also developed wide ranging computer/workstation health programs to help reduce their medical costs and to increase productivity. Some companies, such as S un, have gone further than Blue Cross by developing pamphlets and videos for its employees, and by enabling employees to select a wide range of computer-related equipment, such as articulating keyboard trays, wrist rests, mouse rests, foot rests, back rests, copy stands, telephone headsets, trackballs, glare screens and task lights. Sun created workshops with a physical therapist for small groups of employees. And, more important, Sun's educational materials encouraged peop le to vary their movements and to take periodic short breaks.

Stress, poor posture, relentless work, and poor ergonomics all seem to contribute to RSI. Consequently, a focus on any single item, such as keyboards, is probably misplaced. Even so, few organizations seem ready to equip their staff with office equipment that fits the variety of their bodies, and with effective guidelines for safe work.

COMPUTER SYSTEM SECURITY

In the 1960s and 1970s, the public viewed computer systems as being occasionally unreliable, but basically secure. Recent events publicized in the mass media, as well as Hollywood films, have radically changed that image. The 1983 film *Wargames* depicted a teenage computer-hobbyist, whose intrusion into a U.S. military computer system brought the world to the brink of nuclear war. Although the film's premise is extremely dubious, other military-related computer systems do have serious security problems. In February 1989, eighteen year-old Chicagoan Herbert Zinn, Jr. was sentenced to nine months' imprisonment plus a $10,000 fine for b reaking into U.S. military computers and AT&T computers, and stealing 55 programs.

Clifford Stoll, an astronomer at the University of California's Lawrence Berkeley Labs, started investigating a "hacker" who gained unauthorized access to an account, and used the Berkeley system as a springboard to other (primarily military) computer sys tems.

Over a period of months, Stoll followed the hacker, who entered over 430 computers connected by several networks in the United States and Western Europe. Stoll's book, *The Cuckoo's Egg* provides a fascinating account of the arduous work req uired to locate an intruder's entry point and eventually identify the intruder espionage for the Soviet KGB; reportedly, they gained access to computerized information in NASA headquarters, Los Alamos and Fermilab, along with various U.S. Army computers and military-related computers in Europe.

These examples are particularly serious because they compromise national security, and involve computer systems designed to be open only to a relatively small group of authorized users. Moreover, intrusions may be difficult to detect (and even more diffi cult to trace) because of a multitude of interconnections among electronic networks.

Of course, not all breaches of computer security involve tightly restricted military systems, and not all are marked by malicious intent. In a widely reported episode during early November 1988, Cornell University Computer Science graduate student Robert T. Morris, Jr. planted a "worm" that spread worldwide across several thousand computers linked to a large research computer network (Internet). A small programming miscalculation caused the worm to replicate much faster than the programmer had intende d, necessitating the temporary shutdown of many Internet computers while a "fix" was devised. Aside from this considerable inconvenience to researchers who relied on the computers, and the thousands of hours of technical time to detect and correct the pr oblems, no other damage was done.

But the Internet worm stimulated considerable controversy. Although it was argued that Morris's experiment helped call attention to an important computer security weakness, critics insisted that it was widely known that the Internet was not totally secure. In fact, its gaps were like unlocked house doors in a friendly village. In the critics' view, someone who wandered through unlocked houses and left annoying signs of intrusion dresser drawers, and leaving notes on beds ecurity issues.

Within a month of Morris' worm attack, the Advanced Research Projects Agency (ARPA) announced the establishment of a Computer Emergency Response Team (CERT) to address the computer security concerns of Internet research users. The Coordination Center for the CERT, located at the Software Engineering Institute of the Carnegie Mellon University, taps the expertise of over a hundred computers security experts who work at Internet sites. CERT began issuing advisories about other attacks on Internet sites. Th is Section includes a sample CERT advisory issued in February 1994 after over 10,000 user IDs were compromised by a Trojan login program surreptitiously installed on hundreds of networks linked to the Internet. The modified program, running under Unix, t rapped the first 128 bytes of every login and wrote them to a local file so that the hackers could harvest the passwords.

BALANCING COMPUTER SECURITY AND USABILITY

Security, however, is not the only priority in computer systems: accessibility and ease of use are often competing requirements. As the Cornell Commission pointed out in its comments on the Morris episode:

> A community of scholars should not have to build walls as high as the sky to protect a reasonable expectation of privacy, particularly when such walls will equally impede the free flow of information. A system such as Internet, which provides electronic mail links and data exchange among thousands of researchers around the globe, can be made virtually worthless if security procedures make its operation so cumbersome that people are reluctant or unable to use it.

The same tradeoff confronts millions of microcomputer users, who want easy access to electronic bulletin boards to download software for personal use. Increasingly, they must deal with the possibility that a downloaded program may contain a v irus that is designed to maliciously lock up their system, or erase all the files on their hard disk.

The most emphasized aspect of system security has been the protection of information by prohibiting unauthorized access. Given a sufficient commitment and sufficient precautions (passwords, data encryption, call back systems, restrictions on levels of access, or even physical identification of users and elimination of dial-in access), a reasonably high level of security can be achieved. Like many computer-related issues, "security" has both social and technical dimensions.

Honesty Acknowledging the Risks of Powerful Technologies

It is conventional wisdom that new technologies make daily life more convenient and safer. We could create a vast catalog of improved health technologies, industrial technologies, household technologies, and so forth which fit this maxim. Yet, in the last 20 years, a growing number of well educated people, including scientists and engineers, have become very cautious of blindly accepting new technologies. High profile stories of major environmental hazards, including DDT, fluorocarbons, and toxic spills, as well as stories of how they were pushed by corporate greed and ineptitude have helped shift public opinion.

Computer Scientist Peter G. Neumann argues that we should seek a new common sense with technologies. Neumann draws upon Jerry Mander's environmental ethos and suggests that we apply it to computer technologies as well. His first point — Since most of what we are told about new technology comes from its proponents, be deeply skeptical of all claims — is one that we would take for gra nted in buying a new car or even a house. His second point — Assume all technology 'guilty until proven innocent' — is one that we would normally apply to new drugs. Neumann's article lists all of Mander's ten points. None of them is remarkable, except that we normally don't apply them to assessing new computer technologies. Neumann argues that we should treat computer technologies with the same care that we treat other technologies whose dangers we have come to understand

7

Technological Controversies in Computerisation

This chapter examines social controversies about computerization and ways to computerize that can be more socially beneficial or harmful. Many key questions that people raise about computerization — in their households, communities, workplaces, and so on — refer to possible future events. For example, university librarians may wonder how they should create a computerized "virtual reference desk" for their clients and shift their spending away from paper-based materials. Managers in a software company may w onder how they can best supervise their staffs and foster teamwork if their team members all work in their separate homes in a large urban area. A young man and woman may wonder whether they can send each other romantic letters via electronic mail and ins ure the privacy of their communications. In industrialized societies, millions of professionals and computer specialists ask questions like these very day.

Good answers to questions like these are not always obvious. And thinking through workable answers (and social practices based upon them) can involve a complex web of assumptions about people's rights, the responsibilities of professional to their clients , how people behave, the capabilities of specific technologies, and the nature of ethical behavior. These answers are usually based on a story, however incomplete, about "the future." The time scale of future behavior may be two months away or 10 years aw ay. Most of the key questions about computerization in society focus on future events.

This chapter helps you better understand the unstated but critical social assumptions underlying stories about computerization and changes in social life. Every year thousands of articles and dozens of books comment on the meaning of new computer technol ogies for people, organizations, and society. Much of the literature about computing describes emerging technologies and the ways they expand the limits of the possible. Faster, tinier computers can make it easier for people to find information from the ir homes and hotel rooms, as well as their offices or laboratories.

Larger memories can make more data accessible. Richer display devices, which show lively video, colorful pictures, and text can make interacting with computers more of a reality for mor e people. Emerging higher speed networks can connect thousands of systems, providing communication links only dreamed of a decade ago. The remarkable improvement in the capabilities of computing equipment from one decade to the next excites researchers, d evelopers, and entrepreneurs, as well as the battalions of journalists who document these events in newspapers and magazines.

Yet, although we are frequently told that we are in the midst of a momentous "computer revolution", people who use the term rare ly tell us precisely what it means.

Accounts of the powerful information processing capabilities of computer systems are usually central to many stories of computerization and social change. *Authors write about these changes in technology and social life with different analytical and rhe torical strategies.* Some authors enchant us with images of new technologies that offer exciting possibilities of manipulating large amounts of information rapidly with little effort — to e nhance control, to create insights, to search for information, and to facilitate cooperative work between people.

Terms like "virtual," "smart," and "intelligent" are often sprinkled through these accounts and help give them a buoyant image. Much less fr equently, authors examine a darker social vision when any likely form of computerization will amplify human misery — people sacrificing their freedom to businesses and government agencies, people becoming very dependent on complex technologies that they don't comprehend, and sometimes the image of inadvertent global thermonuclear war.

Both the optimistic and the pessimistic stories of computerization are often crafted with the conventions of utopian and anti-utopian writing. The utopian and anti-utopian genres of social analysis are about 500 years old, and predate the social sciences by about 350 years. Authors who write within these genres examine certain kinds of social possibilities, and usually extrapolate beyond contemporary technologies and social relationships. Utopian tales are devised to stimulate hope in future possibilitie s as well as actions to devise a self-fulfilling prophesy. In contrast, anti-utopian tales are devised to stimulate anger at horrible possibilities and actions to avoid disaster.

Although utopian visions often serve important roles in giving people a positive sense of direction, they can mislead when their architects exaggerate the likelihood of easy and desirable social changes. We are particularly interested in what can be learn ed, and how we can be misled, by a particular brand of utopian thought ral enabling element of a utopian vision. Sometimes people will casually refer to exotic technologies s. It refers to analyses in which the use of specific technologies plays a key role in shaping a utopian social vision in which their use easily makes life enchanting and liberating for nearly everyone.

In contrast, *technological anti-utopianism* examines how certain broad families of technology facilitate a social order that is relentlessly harsh, destructive, and miserable. This section includes articles by Weiland, Stewart and Kelly which illustrate technological utopianism and articles by Birkerts and Winner which illustrate technological anti-utopianism. Technological utopianism is particularly influential in North America and often influences writing about new technologies.

Authors craft utopian and anti-utopian writings within a set of conventions that limit what they say. Even though these writings describe possible future events and social forms, their conventions prevent the authors from discussing important social rel ationships that are also likely. These utopian and anti-utopian writings about computerization form a *genre* of discourse. A genre refers to any body of work that is shaped by a set of conventions. The works that we readily identify as romantic come dies, impressionist paintings, horror films, newspaper editorials, and popular movie reviews are constructed with a set of conventions that make them readily intelligible and accessible. Authors and artists who work wholly within the conventions of a genr e also limit the kinds of themes that they can effectively examine. Authors of romantic comedies usually don't explore boredom between the romantic partners and the ways that they negotiate their differences, day to day.

This chapter examines how genre formulas influence writing about computerization which is supposed to be nonfictional — writing in which the author attempts to tell us truths about the world of computerization "out there" and not simply the author's imag ination. Many science fiction writers portray very vivid technologically utopian and anti-utopian images. But journalists, managers, and computer scientists also organize their stories about computerization in utopian terms in allegedly nonfiction outlets such as *IEEE Spectrum, Communications of the ACM, Scientific American* and the *New York Times*.

A few of these works, including Weiland's selection about meetings with desktop conferencing systems, are framed in terms of future technologies and related social practices. But many descriptions of the use of current technologies in existing setting s are also framed with specific genre conventions. Conventions make works more easily intelligible to their primary audiences. And social analyses of computing are written with genre conventions that limit the kinds of ideas that can be readily examined. Many professionals and scholars who read these social analyses are often unaware of the ways that works are crafted within the conventions of specific genres, and the ways in that these conventions limit as well as facilitate analysis and debate.

Technological Utopianism in Visions of Specific Contexts

Many of the books and articles which are infused with technological utopianism focus on some specific segment of society — such as home, schools, factories, or libraries, or upon specific technologies — such as computer networks or virtual reality.

A Meetings Odyssey" by Ross Weiland examines how new forms of virtual video conferencing might enable people to have cross-country business meetings from their desktops. Or they might even videoconference from their bedrooms an d appear in business clothes to everyone else who is tuned in. Weiland vividly portrays a way that this technology might be used, and emphasizes the benefits of this technology and others that he expects to see developed in the next decade. But he mention s potential problems in these words:

While the techno-types are working to perfect a brand-new field of applied science, sociologists worry about the human element: What about the loss of human contact? What about the employer's enhanced capability to monitor a person's work? Such concerns may well slow the acceptance of desktop videoconferencing. But like the fax and the PC before it, we will embrace this technology in the near future and ask a familiar question: How did we do business without it?

A picture, even a live-action video, may never substitute for a site inspection. But imagine using these capabilities to conduct a meeting from your desk. Wouldn't you think twice if the alternative were an arduous and costly trip by air?

One of the distinctive features of Weiland's analysis is illustrated in this brief excerpt. He mentions potential problems of desktop conferencing, such as tightening surveillance over people's activities at work. But he doesn't examine them seriously. R ather he trivializes them into minor worries that people will just "get over." People who have become accustomed to new technologies often won't want to return to older forms: inevitably the refrigerator replaces the ice box, the flush toilet replaces t he outhouse, the computerized word processor and spell checker replace the typewriter and pen, and so on. But many technological advances are not simple substitutions.

For example, we did not simply replace horses and mules with cars and trucks. We have c onfigured an elaborate system of motorized transport, including new roads, traffic regulations, gas stations, repair shops, insurance, and so on. In many cities, cars come first, and pedestrians come second.

But many city planners have been finding ways t o design downtowns, shopping centers, and residential neighborhoods so that people can walk, drive cars or even bicycle without feeling unsafe. One hallmark of Weiland's technological utopianism is his unwillingness to acknowledge and examine how desktop conferencing can be done badly, and how deploying these technologies in a humane way may entail important kinds of social designs as well as hot technologies. Weiland's analysis is but one illustration of technological utopianism. There are some importan t technological utopian analysis which emphasize a good life for almost all participants, for example, by democratizing access to important technologies such as computer networks.

Thomas Stewart illustrates how technological utopian themes can appear in news magazines and business magazines such as *Time, Fortune* and *Business Week*. Stewart published, "Boom Time on the New Frontier: Growth of Co mputer Networks" in *Fortune,* a major business magazine, in 1993. In contrast with Weiland, Stewart focusses upon emerging trends for which he can provide concrete examples today:

> The future of information technology descends upon us in a swarm of buzzwords: global village, electronic superhighway, information age, electronic frontier. Someday soon, cyberspace — the vast, intangible territory where computers meet and exchange information — will be populated with electronic communities and businesses.
>
> In your home, a protean box will hook you into a wealth of goods and services. It will receive and send mail, let you make a phone or video call or send a fax o r watch a movie or buy shoes or diagnose a rash or pay bills or get cash (a new digital kind) or write your mother. That will be just the living-room manifestation of what promises to be a radical — and rapid — transformation of commerce and society , the greatest since the invention of the automobile.
>
> The process has already begun. In Japan, used-car dealers gather via their computers on Saturday mornings to take part in an electronic auction, buying and selling cars by pressing the button on a joystick. In New York City, a seller of su rgical gauze and other medical disposables recently logged on to a global electronic bulletin board operated by the World Trade Center and found a supplier in China. Now, instead of buying from U.S. wholesalers, he sells to them. The largest market in

the world — the trillion or so dollars a day in international currency transactions — runs almost entirely over networks.

During the next few years, electronic markets will grow and begin operating over cheap, accessible public networks — the so-called electronic highway. Just as railroads opened the West, the highway will open wide the electronic frontier. Whole industries will be destroyed and new ones born; productivity will leap and competitive advantage shift in the direction of small business.

The technological utopianism is not simply signalled by Stewart's buoyant optimism about the growth of "electronic commerce" and growth of services on the Internet. It is marked by his failure to carefully engage critical questions about t he downsides of the explosion of excitement over computer networks. He starts by noting the flurry of buzzwords that journalists, technologists, and scholars use in discussions of computer networking: global village, electronic superhighway, information age, and electronic frontier. But he then quickly picks up "cyberspace" and launches his analysis of emerging trends and significant examples.

Stewart's article builds on the recent and growing public popularity of the Internet in the United States. President Bill Clinton and Vice President Al Gore stimulated substantial interest in computer networks (and the Internet) through their promotion of "information superhighways" — or, The National Information Infrastructure (NII). In 1992, most professionals outside of the computer industry, research institutes, and academia had never heard of the Internet. By 1994, many people who didn't know what the Internet was wanted accounts to access it so that they wouldn't be left out. Bookstores that carried a few books about services on the Internet soon devoted whole shelves to the topic. Many of these books are rather practical guidebooks that describe diverse services (such as e mail, LISTSERVs, gopher, ftp, and World Wide Web) and inform readers about specific examples and some pragmatics of using specific software. These books are generally buoyant about network services, but are not structured within technologically utopian co nventions. While they encourage people to try out the Internet, they don't promise people that widescale network use will eliminate social ills such as street crime, social isolation, lifelong poverty, and unemployment! But people often turn to them afte r their interest has been piqued by articles such as Stewart's.

It is unfortunate that the executive branch of United States federal government has not been a good source of studies which help us understand the possibilities — but also the dilemmas and social choices - of a society which depends as much upon computer networks for daily services as we have come to depend upon the motorized transport system for cars, busses, and trucks. For example, a recent federal report about the NII discusses the ways that "improvem ents in the technical foundation upon which modern communications rests can benefit all Americans." This report relentlessly focusses upon applications of computer networking to applications like digital libraries, life-long learning, manufac turing and commercial transactions. The authors of this report, emphasize the way that the widespread expansion of computer networks can vitalize numerous aspects of business activity and social life in the United States. Like Weiland and Stewart they o ccasionally mention potential problems, and then rapidly skate by them.

Utopian Social Visions

Utopian thinkers portray whole societies whose members live very ideal lives. The first such description appeared in Plato's *Republic*, written some 2500 years ago. But the name "Utopia" derives from Thomas More, who in 1516 published a story about an ideal society vation. More's fanciful name, which literally meant "nowhere," has been picked up and applied to a whole tradition of writing and thinking about the forms of society that would supposedly make many people happiest.

There have been hundreds of utopian blueprints. They differ substantially in their details: some have focused on material abundance as the key to human happiness while other have advanced ideal visions of austerity and simplicity. Some utopian thinkers advocate private property as a central social institution, while alternative visions place a premium on shared property.

The most obvious utopian sources are discourses which the authors explicitly identify as fictional accounts, complete with traditional devices such as invented characters and fanciful dialogue. But here we are concerned with discourses about computerizat ion which authors present as primarily realistic or factual accounts (and which are cataloged as non-fiction in bookstores and libraries).

Utopian images permeate the literatures about computerization in society. After all, the United States was founded on premises that were utopian in the 1700s. The Declaration of Indepen dence asserts that "all men are created equal" and that they would be guaranteed the right to "life, liberty, and the pursuit of happiness". This sentiment stood in significant contrast to the political cultures of the European monarchies of the time, w here the rule of the king or queen, along with nobles (most of whom were "elected" by heredity) determined people's fates. Of course, asserting the right to "life, liberty, and the pursuit of happiness" as universal didn't immediately make it so. Until 1 865, for example, slaves were legally property, and could be bought and sold, told where to live, and broken apart from their families. Women were not allowed to vote until 1919. And even in 1963, Martin Luther King's major speech about a country free of racial discrimination was called "I Have a Dream" Furthermore utopian ideals are hard to put into practice. Their advocates often have to fight hard to change social practices to better fit their ideals.

The United States broke free of the English Crown through a four year war. Almost two hundred year s later, Martin Luther King and others advanced the cause of improved civil rights in the United States through aggressive confrontations: marches, rallies, court injunctions and sit-ins, as well as through more quiet persuasion. The resulting social cha nges, which altered the balance of privilege and exploitation, did not come quietly and peacefully. Nor have the utopian dreams of our nation's founders been fully achieved after two hundred years of struggle.

Visions of Computerized Societies

Technological utopian accounts that focus on some specific area of social life, such as desktop conferencing or electronic commerce. The classical utopian writings were much more expansive since their authors examined whole societies, and discussed leisure as well as work, child rearing as well as schooling, and so on. There are some relatively broad technological utopian accounts that focus upon computerization. But more frequently, we find powerful images that link computeriza tion and social change characterized with sweeping terms like "computer revolution", "information society", and "intelligent machine." These catch phrases have strong metaphorical associations, and are often introduced by authors to advance positive, ex citing images of computerization.

"The Electronic Hive" by Kevin Kelly illustrates this more expansive, and almost poetic writing. Kelly's essay is drawn from his recent book, *Out of Control: The Rise of Neo-biological Civilization* which examines how emerging c omputer technologies may develop like biological collectives — beehives. Kelly examines some parallels that he sees between bee colonies and computer networks, especially the groups of people who use the Internet. Kelly argues that huma nity is moving to a new stage of technological co-evolution with decentralized systems, like the Internet and that computer networks provide new opportunities for people to deepen their communications with others. The techn ological utopianism of Kelly's essay (and his much longer book) is constructed from the troubling questions that he ignores as well as from the buoyant themes and examples that he examines explicitly.

Kelly writes about the epochal changes in whole societies, much like George Gilder and Alvin Toffler. Alvin Toffler's best seller of he early 1980s, *The Third Wave,* helped stimulate popular enthusiasm for computerization. Toffler characterized maj or social transformations in terms of large shifts in the organization of society, driven by technological change.

The "Second Wave" was the shift from agricultural societies to industrial societies. Toffler contrasts industrial ways of organizing societ ies to new social trends that he links to computer and microelectronic technologies. He is masterful employing succinct breathless prose to suggest major social changes. He also invented terminology to help characterize some of these social changes rms like "second wave", "third wave", "electronic cottage", "infosphere", "technosphere", "prosumer", "intelligent environment", etc. Many of Toffler's new terms did not become commonly accepted. Even so, they help frame a seductive description of progr essive social change stimulated by new technologies. The breathless enthusiasm can be contagious er the ways that people perceive information, the kinds of information they can get easily, how they handle the information they get, and the forms of social life that we develop. Yet these accounts often caricature key answers by using only illustration s that support their generally buoyant theses. And they skillfully sidestep tough questions while creating a sense of excitement about the new.

Technological Anti-Utopianism

Some important writings about the social changes linked to computerization criticize utopian assumptions. In fact, some authors articulate a comparably dark "anti-utopian" view of computerization.

Joseph Weizenbaum, in his popular book, *Computer Power and Human Reason*, observes:

Our society's growing reliance on computer systems that were initially intended to "help" people make analyses and decisions, but which have long since surpassed the understanding of their users and become indispensable to them is a very serious d evelopment. First, decisions are made with the aid of, and sometimes entirely by, computers whose programs no one any longer knows explicitly or understand since no one can know the criteria or rules on which such decisions are based. Second, the rules a nd criteria that are embedded in such computer systems become immune to change, because, in the absence of detailed understanding of the inner workings of a computer system, any substantial modification of it is very likely to render the whole system inop erable and possibly unrestorable. Such computer systems can therefore only grow. And their growth and the increasing reliance placed on them is then accompanied by an increasing legitimation of their "knowledge base."

Weizenbaum criticizes visions of computerized databases which record historical data because they usually eliminate important information which is too complex or costly to include:

The computer has thus begun to be an instrument for the destruction of history. For when society legitimates only those "data" that are in one standard format, then history, memory itself, is annihilated. *The New York Times* has already beg un to build a "data bank" of current events. Of course, only those data that are easily derivable as by-products of typesetting machines are admissible to the system. As the number of subscribers to this system grows, as they learn to rely more and more upon "all the news that [was once] fit to print," as the *Times* proudly identifies its editorial policy, how long will it be before what counts as fact is determined by the system, before all other knowledge, all memory, is simply declared illegitimate? Soon a supersystem will be built, based on *The New York Times'* data bank (or one very much like it), from which "historians" will make inferences about what "really" happened, about who is connected to whom, and about the "real" logic of events.

Weizenbaum's observations gain more force when one realizes that journalists often don't simply report "the facts". They tend to rely upon standard kinds of sources, voices of publicly legitimate authority, in framing stories. For example, when a univers ity alters a curriculum, deans and professors are more likely than students are to appear in the resulting news story.

Gaye Tuchman characterized reporters in search of a story as casting a selective "newsnet" around their favorite kinds of sources. Jou rnalists often don't cast their nets to give equal voice to all kinds of informed parties. While reporters are much more likely to go to "the grass roots" today than they were in the 1950s, each newspaper prints a mix of stories in a style that reflects a relatively stable character. Even if the mastheads were interchanged, one would not confuse *The New York Times* with a small town weekly newspaper.

Moreover, Weizenbaum speaks with authority about future events ("Soon a supersystem will be built . . ."). Without special design, nothing in the database technology itself would be likely to give the user a clue about its real limitations in representin g a narrow range of perspectives. Nonetheless, the convenience of database technology makes it ver y tempting for others to rely on it as a primary source, without appreciating its shortcomings. That is the cautionary note that one might draw from Weizenbaum's bitter observations.

But Weizenbaum's argument is primarily polemical. He doesn't discuss any virtues of news databases, or conditions under which they might not have the deleterious consequences he identifies. After all, news databases can substantially assist in useful re search as long as they do not become a sole source of information.

Sven Birkerts essay "The Electronic Hive - Refuse It" comes from his larger book *The Gutenberg Elegies: The Fate of Reading in the Electronic Age*. Birkerts' essay serves as a vivid counterpoint to Kevin Kelly's essay by criticizing as alienating the kind of enmeshment in nets that Kelly finds so satisfying. Birkerts is particularly concerned that humanly meaningful events and experiences are most-often anchored in human-scale and bodily experiences. While we can send messages acr oss a computer net in a few seconds, or even milliseconds, we don't have meaningful conversations or meaningful life experiences in seconds or milliseconds. Computer networks can be seductive places to work, play and communicate. But Birkirts views them a s further removing people from their natural worlds, much as life in the largest paved and built up cities have removed us from the rhythms and textures of the natural world. Where Kelly sees computer networks as deepening people's humanity, Birkerts sees them as fundamentally alienating.

Langdon Winner's short description of worklife in electronic offices ("Electronic Office: Playpen or Prison") serves as a counterpoint to Weiland's essay about desktop conferencing, as well as to Kelly's essay about the new freedom's of computer networks. Winner distinguishes three classes of participants: technical professionals, ordinary workers, and upper managers. His brief vignette indicates that each group experiences different kinds of work worlds. The technical professionals are likely to have sig nificant freedom in maneuvering through computer networks and communicating with their co-workers. He claims that "ordinary workers," (who seem to be primarily clerical), are highly regimented and that their performance is tightly monitored through comput erized control systems. Last, upper managers sit outside of these computer networks, and constrain their workers within them.

Winner echoes Birkerts' concern that people will be further alienated through the use of computer networks through his sarcastic characterization of technical professionals —

They experience computer networks as spheres of democratic or even anarchic activity. Especially for those ill at ease in the physical presence of others (a feeling not uncommon among male engineers), the phenomenon of disembodied space seems to offer comfort and fulfillment. Here are new opportunities for self-express ion, creativity, and a sense of mastery! Some begin to feel they are most alive, most free when wandering through the networks; they often "disappear" into them for days on end.

Technological anti-utopians craft tragedies that serve as counterpoints to the technological utopians inspiring romances. Technological anti utopianism is a particular form of cultural criticism which portrays the troublesome potentials of new technologies as relentlessly harsh. For example, both Birkerts and Winner acknowledge that people may enjoy playing with and communicating through compu ter networks. But they portray them as superficial seductions which suck the life from people's souls — much like heroin.

Conventions of Technological Utopianism and anti-Utopianism

Utopian and anti-utopian analysts paint their portraits of computerization with monochromatic brushes: white or black. The anti-utopians' characterizations of the tragic possibilities of computerization provide an essential counterbalance to the giddy-hea ded optimism of the utopian accounts. The romances and tragedies are not all identical. For example, some anti-utopian writings examine the possibilities of computerized systems for coercion, while others emphasize alienation. But the utopian and anti-uto pian genres have some important inherent limitations

It is simply unclear how a social group can move from where it is to the more utopian social order. Unfortunately, computer specialists f social assumptions. Nor are computer specialists taught to understand the dynamics of social change. Utopian visions are sometimes characterized as "reality transcending". They play important roles in stimulating hope and giving people a positive sense of direction. But they can mislead when their architects exaggerate the lik elihood of easy and desirable social changes. Writing about technological utopianism in the 1930s, Wilson, Pilgrim and Tasjian comment:

> Belief in the limitless future potential of the machine had both its positive and negative aspects. During the 1930s this almost blind faith in the power of the machine to make the world a better place helped hold a badly shattered nation toge ther. ... These science fiction fantasies contributed to an almost naive approach to serious problems and a denial of problems that could already be foreseen.

In any of its forms, technological utopianism can be exciting and expand the range of people's visions of what is possible.

"Utopia confronts reality not with a measured assessment of the possibilities of change but with the demand for change. This is the way the world should be. It refuses to accept current definitions of the possible because it knows these to be a pa rt of the reality it seeks to change. In its guise as utopia, by the very force of its imaginative presentation, it energizes reality, infusing it ... with "the power of the new."

But in characterizing "a world that should be," technological utopians embed specific commitments to ways of life within their visions. Ross Weiland expressed his enthusiasm for desktop video conferencing in terms that trivialized any serious discussion of the ways of living and working with and without these technologies. Some of his comments here:

While the techno-types are working to perfect a brand-new field of applied science, sociologists worry about the human element: What about the loss of human contact? What about the employer's enhanced capability to monitor a person's wo rk? Such concerns may well slow the acceptance of desktop videoconferencing. But like the fax and the PC before it, we will embrace this technology in the near future and ask a familiar question: How did we do business without it?

We can extract a set of Weiland' s demands from this brief passage: ignore the possible loss of human contact; ignore the employer's enhanced capability to monitor a person's work; embrace desktop videoconferencing soon not do business without it.

The actual uses and consequences of developing computer systems depend upon the "way the world works". Conversely, computerized systems may slowly, but inexorably, change "the way the world works" w to understand the social opportunities and dilemmas of computerization without becoming seduced by the social simplifications of utopian romance, or becoming discouraged by anti-utopian nightmares. Both kinds of images are far too simplified. But they do serve to help identify an interesting and important set of social possibilities.

Anti-utopian writings are far less numerous in the United States. They serve as an important counterbalance to technological utopianism. But they could encourage a comparably ineffective sense of despair and inaction. Utopian and anti-utopian visions embo dy extreme assumptions about technology and human behavior. But their causal simplicity gives them great clarity and makes them easy to grasp — to enjoy or to abhor. They can resonate with our dreams or nightmares. Consequently, they have immense influen ce in shaping the discussions (and real directions) of computerization.

Writings in each genre have formulaic limits much in the way that romantic fiction (or any other literary genre) has important limits. Caweltinotes that "The moral fantasy of the romance is that of love triumphant and permanent, ove rcoming all obstacles and difficulties." This does not mean that we can't be entertained or our appreciation of life enriched by romantic fictions; it is simply a genre with important formulaic limits. The moral fantasies of technolo gical utopianism and anti-utopianism similarly limit the way that they can teach us about the likely social realities of new forms of computerization: one is romantic and the other is tragic.

The Social Production of Technologically Utopian Materials

Technological utopian and anti-utopian analyses of computing do not "just appear" in journals, magazines, and books. Their production and publication has some social organization, although not a simple one. Firms marketing their services and products thr ough advertisements, product brochures, and broadcasting is one kind of large-scale social process which couples utopian imagery and computerization. Typical business journalism is also a systematic source.

Let's take a simple journalistic example. The editorial staff of a business magazine may agree that an article about the ways that work is changing in "virtual offices' would appeal to an important segment of readers. The reporter might have a few weeks t o read some background materials and contact a set of people who might be plausible experts for more details and lively quotes before she writes her story. She might develop a list which includes managers firms which have reputedly created reduced their p hysical office space and created some virtual offices, consultants who advise about these business practices, and professors who are developing advanced versions of possibly relevant technologies, such as computer conferencing systems. Many of these infor mants have an interest in putting a positive spin on virtual offices. If the managers are willing to be quoted, they would like their firms to appear well managed in the magazine story. The professors believe in the potential contributions of their techno logies, and would like to stimulate more interest in them. So they will also emphasize interesting ways to organize with them. The consultants might like their names in the article to help stimulate new business for them. They have an interest in suggest ing that virtual offices can be tricky to organize well, but that they can be good and productive workplaces with the right consultant on-hand to provide wise advice. The reporter, would like to publish an engaging story and business reporters often seem to push for short vivid quotes (sometimes called soundbites in television).

Business reporters often produce stories with a technologically-utopian spin, like the selection by Stewart about electronic commerce, out of a research process like this. It's an exciting story about a possible business trend. The reporter will usually s trive to construct the story within a frame that readers can readily grasp. Technological utopianism and technological anti-utopianism are two such frames whose conventions readers can readily grasp.

In addition to advertising and journalism, there is a third important large scale social process that results in numerous books and articles about computerization that are framed in technologically utopian terms. "Computerization movements" refer to loos ely organized collections of groups that promote specific forms of computerization, such as computer networking or instructional computing.

Computerization movements are like other kinds of movements that engage people in diverse organized activities with an interest in gaining broader support: political movements, like the civil rights movement; art movements, like surrealism; religious mov ements, like fundamentalist Christianity. Certainly, political, art, and religious movements differ in their public goals, the ways that they recruit members, their collective activities and so on. But they share important commonalities. They also give us insights into sources of technologically utopian and anti-utopian writings written by professionals (in addition to ad copy and journalism). "Computerization Movements and Tales of Technological Utopianism," Suzanne Iacono examine these sources in some detail. Two computerization movements — computer based education and computer networking. But we could have examined other computerization movements as well, such as those which promote digital libraries or artificial intelligence. One of the surprising aspects of our analysis is that we treat these tec hnologies as the products of social movements rather than only as the products of research labs and industrial firms.

Technological utopian and anti-utopian visions embody extreme assumptions about technology and human behavior. They portray new technologies as either extremely pure and innocent or as hopelessly corrupting. But the simplicity of these storylines gives them great clarity and makes them easy to grasp rections) of computerization.

The year 2000, there will be a large market for social analyses of computerization stimulated by:

- the steady stream of computing innovations;
- the drive by academic computer science departments and Federal funding agencies to justify large expenditures on computing research;
- justifications for major national computerization programs, such as expanding the National Information Infrastructure; and
- articles examining life and technology in the 21st century.

Many social analyses of computing that appear in popular and professional magazines, as well as in newspapers and the trade press, will be strongly influenced by technologically utopian assumptions. Consequently, sophisticated professionals and researche rs should be specially aware of the strengths and limitations of this genre of analysis.

Beyond Technological Utopianism and Anti-Utopianism

These quotations introduce some of the controversies about the visions of computerization: To what extent are utopian or anti-utopian visions helpful in understanding the social possibilities of computerization? To what extent is social real ism a more interesting and reliable guide to the future than the more utopian or anti-utopian visions? If one doesn't trust the anti-utopian or utopian visions, how does one develop a broad framework for asking questions about *what should be done* Attractive alternatives to utopian and anti-utopian analyses should be more credible in characterizing conflict in a social order, the distribution of knowledge, the ways of solving problems that arise from new technologies. They should rest upon less det erministic logics of social change. Most important, they would identify the social contingencies that make technologies (un)workable and social changes that are benign or harmful for diverse groups.

"Social realism" refers to a genre which uses empirical data to examines computerization as it is actually practiced and experienced. Social realists write their articles and books with a tacit label: *"I have carefully observed and examin ed computerization in some key social settings and I will tell you how it really is."* The most common methods are those of journalism and the social sciences, such as critical inquiries, and ethnography. But the genre is best characterized by the efforts of authors to communicate their understanding of computerization as it "really works" based on reporting fine grained empirical detail. Social realism gains its force through gritty observations about the social worlds in which computer system s are used.

Social realist analyses often acknowledge complex patterns of social conflict, and yet are more open-ended and contingent than both genres of utopian analysis. In the following sections of this book, you will find many social realist analyses of computerization.

8

Internet Governance

The Internet Corporation for Assigned Names and Numbers (ICANN) was created in 1998 to perform technical coordination of the Internet. ICANN also lays the foundations for governance, creating capabilities for promulgating and enforcing global regulations on Internet use. ICANN leverages the capabilities in the Internet domain name system (DNS) to implement four mechanisms of governance: authority, law, sanctions, and jurisdictions. These governance-related features are embodied in seemingly technical features of ICANN's institutional design. Recognition of ICANN's governance mechanisms allows us to better understand the Internet's emerging regulatory regime.

The Internet has often been hailed as a domain of be nevolentanarchy, a place where free communication is securely in place. It is a "modern Hydra" capable of circumvent in regulation and a" space of no control". As Internetbard John Perry Barlow says, "Governments of the Industrial World, . . . You have no sovereignty where we gather".

Stated less colourfully, the Internet presents challenges to governance. By governance, the existence of some authority able to make globally applicable rules for Un receptive May 2000; accepted 13 August 2001. Research for this study was performed while the author was a resident at the Center for the Sociology of Innovation at the Ecole desMines, Paris, with support from a Chateaubri and Fellowship from the French Embassy in the United States.

The reasons for this lie both in characteristics of the technology, which make control difficult, and in the global reach of Internet communications, which creates jurisdiction all conflict among government regulators. This "ungovernability " of the Internet, however, is changing. In his book *Code*, Lawrence Lessig documents various strategies to eliminate user anonymity and there by facilitate law enforcement. Likewise, in a recent court case over Internet auctions of Nazi memorabilia that was illegal in France, the Yahoo! Corporation was ordered to detect viewer's location and apply local content regulations to them. As with other technologies spreceding it, as the Internet becomes important to the society around it, attempts are made to integrate it with in existing regulatory structures.

The most significant development in the trend to render the Internet governable is the creation of the Internet Corporation for Assigned Names and Numbers (ICANN). Created in 1998, ICANN is a private, nonprotentity whose official mandate is to perform technical coordination of core Internet resources, most notably domain names (e.g., mycomputer.org). Its site of incorporation lies in California but its authority extends, directly or indirectly, overall users of the Internet.

ICANN has the potential to radically change the nature of the Internet. By putting in place all the mechanisms needed for the creation, promulgation, and enforcement of regulations, ICANN makes effective Internet governance possible for the first time. No longer is the Internet a Hydra that is impossible to control. ICANN's mechanisms for governance can serve any number of possible regulations. The frequency of past attempts to regulate the Internet suggests that the realization of these mechanisms could attract widespread interest in their utilization.

Depending on one's viewpoint, creation of a capability for governance holds the promise or the threat of taming the electronic frontier. For peacemakers and Internet users, this account can help inform policy. That the Internet has a point of central control and that ICANN makes global public policy possible are not widely admitted. Recognition of these governance capabilities justies the application of normative criteria of legitimacy, accountability, and equity to the institution and its processes. This study contributes to a growing body of policy literature that analyses ICANN from the perspective of its historical origins, its legal status, and its institutional design.

This account is also relevant to theoretical debates over the relationship between technological systems and their social context. Recent scholarship in the social construction of technology has emphasized the influence of social factors in shaping technological change. Writers on technology policy have likewise emphasized how designing systems is comparable to writing law, insofar as both activities create social structures that constrain human behaviour. ICANN offers stark evidence of such social structuring, with the domain name system defining important parameters of governance. In what follows, first consider the technological and institutional factors that have inhibited Internet regulation and then continue with a more general discussion of what governance is. Then examine the domain name system, both as a technological and administrative hierarchy, and characteristics that allow for governance. There then follows an analysis of the mechanisms of Internet governance as realized in ICANN. Then, as an illustration of how the governance mechanisms work inpractice.

The Problem of Internet Governance

Regardless of whether one supports or opposes special regulations, it is generally recognized that regulation of the Internet has proven difficult. Copying music, software, and other forms of intellectual property has become simple, and the growth in legal actions against property violators likely represents only a small fraction of incidents of unauthorized copying. Attempts by national governments to control content have foundered on the Internet's global nature and the inter jurisdictional conflicts in regulation.

Barriers to regulation arise in part from characteristics of the technology. Internet communications do not pass through a central channel but are instead passed between many independent networks, and even the messages themselves are broken into packets that may follow different itineraries from source to destination. With multiple independent parties sending multiple independent packets through multiple independent channels, there is no central communication channel that could serve as a control point for promulgating and enforcing regulations.

Regulation also founders on institutional factors. The Internet challenges established jurisdictions. Public authority resides in the state, whose foundational characteristic is the exercise control over a geographically defined domain. Yet the "spaceless" nature of the Internet violates the geographical underpinning of public authority. The mismatch between a network that is global and regulations that are national under mines many attempts at regulation. To make conceptual sense of this situation, it is useful to step back from the details and consider governance from a theoretical level. What is governance? What is needed in order to govern? What is needed for governance of the Internet?

In *Democracy and Its Critics,* Robert Dahl defines what governance is and what is needed to achieve it. He identies a set of "assumptions of a political order" that specify the minimal conditions for a system of governance. The first is an *authority* Governance requires a governor or a sovereign. An entity, be it an individual or a group, must make policy decisions that apply to the members of the polity. A second governance mechanism is *law*. Laws implement policy decisions. They might take the form of a tax, a license, or simply a binding rule. Third, there must be some mechanism for imposing sanctions. This allows for punishment of those who violate laws. Finally, governance requires the definition of jurisdiction. Jurisdiction defines the space over which the authority makes decisions and within which the laws apply and are enforced by the threat of sanctions. These four mechanisms make governance possible: the governing *authority* can make a policy decision that applies within its jurisdiction, embodying that decision in *law* and imposing sanctions on whomever disobeys. The Internet's vaunted ungovernability results from the absence of these four mechanisms. Regulation is difficult because authority, law, sanctions, and jurisdictions are noting place. ICANN realizes these four mechanisms through its control of the Internet's domain name system (DNS). Although Internet communication has no central control point, Internet addressing, as realized in the DNS, is centralized. DNS provides the control point from which to regulate users. Moreover, the DNS is also an essential resource, so it provides a means of sanctioning users: denial of access to domain names is the equivalent to banishment from the Internet. The DNS also defines jurisdictions on the Internet. The logical organization of the DNS allows authority to be mapped onto distinct zones. Finally, the contractual foundations of the DNS provide opportunities to promulgate regulations. Taken together, these features render ICANN capable of governance.

In order to understand ICANN, one must first understand the domain name system. The Internet really consists of two "systems," one for communications (the" TCP/IP" protocols) and one for addressing (the DNS). The communication system is the Internet as we commonly know it. It is extremely decentralized—so much so that it is really not a "system" at all but rather just a set of protocols by which independent computer networks can send data packets to each other. It is this decentralized system that informs most public understanding of the Internet and that underlies claims about ungovernability.

In marked contrast to this, the addressing system—the domain name system (DNS)—is centralized. Nearly all Internet communications rely on this single system. The DNS can be thought of as the Internet's telephone book and directory assistance service. Before one computer can communicate with another, it must do the equivalent of contacting directory assistance with a name of the party it wishes to call and receiving back the number to dial. This is a necessary prelude to communication.

Internally, the DNS consists of a database and a dynamic look up service. The database includes pairs of domain names and IP numbers. Domain names are alphanumeric (and hence human-friendly) identiers of computers on the Internet. IP (Internet Protocol) numbers (or addresses) are machine-friendly numeric identiers. For example, a given computer's domain name might be mycomputer.org, and its corresponding IP number might be 12.34.56.78. The DNS resolves domain names into IP numbers. In name resolution, the DNS accepts a domain name from a user and returns the corresponding number. The DNS computers performing name resolution are called *name servers. Only* after resolution has occurred can the user-to-user e-mail or web communication begin.

This two-step procedure is immediately visible on most web browsers (e.g., Net scape Navigator). Once a user enters a domain name, the browser will indicate that it is interacting with the DNS by posting a message like "Looking up host . . ." As long as a few seconds may pass before resolution is performed, and IP number is returned, and actual communication may begin. Sometimes name resolution fails, as when a misspelled name generates an error message like, "Unable to locate host . . . ," and no number is returned. By watching the status messages on a browser's screen, a user can observe the name resolution process. At the heart of the DNS is the Internet's *name space*. The name space lists (nearly) all computers on the Internet. At the time of this writing the name space contains tens of millions of entries. When one reads statistics about the growth of the Internet, the numbers usually refer to the size of the name space. It provides a rough approximation of the number of individual users: Since most computers listed in the DNS are gateways into private networks with many users, the number of users is much greater than the number of entries in the name space.

In a manner of speaking, the name space *is* the Internet. In order to exist on the Internet, a computer must be listed in the name space. Without a listing (without a domain name and an IP number) a computer cannot be found by others. Removal of a computer's listing from the name space constitutes a kind of banishment, for a computer disappears from the list of addressable computers. Whatever entity controls the name space database effectively controls the Internet. These points are discussed in detail next.

As currently designed, the name space must obey certain design principles. The system's designers claim that the name space must be unique and it must be managed by a single entity. There can only be one database that constitutes the definitive listing of computers on the Internet. Copies may exist, but in dependent name spaces cannot, because they could evolve to have different contents. Were multiple, independent names paces to exist, a given domain name could resolve to different IP addresses depending on which name space was used, which would render communication unreliable. This technologica l imperative of uniqueness underlies the centrality of the DNS, for all communications must use a single, authoritative name space. The Internet's use of a unique name space (with a single administrator) "is a technical necessity, not a policy choice". (Were this design feature not necessary, then numerous possibilities for policy choices would be opened).

Administration

DNS is more than a technical system; it is also an administrative and policy system. Continuing with our simplied view of DNS as a single, non distribute d database, we can examine the DNS in terms of a single administrator and a single policy authority. The *policy authority* entity makes general rules for changes to the name space, such as allowable domain names, cost of registration in the name space, and restrictions on the addition or deletion of names. The administrator implements these decisions, adding, deleting, and modifying the database entries to reflect the entry, exit, and changed status of computers. The administrator also ensures the reliable operation of the name server.

The DNS's uniqueness requirement means that the policy authority and the administrator exercise monopoly power. There must be a unique name space, and it must be managed by a unique administrator, who, in turn, must be subject to a unique policy authority. "Both the design and the implementation of the DNS protocol are heavily based on the assumption that there is a single owner ormaintainer". Only in this way can the name space be guaranteed to function reliably. Directly or indirectly, this one DNS administrator contracts with every network connected to the Internet. Thus, paralleling the DNS's technical centralization is administrative and policy centralization.

The DNS administrator is also called a *registry*. For a computer to be available on the Internet, the user must approach the administrator and request to be *registered. The* registry registers the computer by adding the user's name–number pair to the name space. The legal mechanism used to connect the central policy authority with users is the *contrac*t. The Internet is a network of networks; most computers registered in the name space are gateways to private networks managed by net work administrators. Each listing in the DNS is accompanied by a contract between the central DNS administrator and a *network administrato*r.

The contract species rules and conditions for inclusion in the name space, such as the provision of contact information, the payment of an annual fee, acknowledgment of the role of the DNS adaministrator, and so on. Thus, every network in the Internet has a contract with the single entity overseeing the DNS. These contracts implement policy centralization. In this simplied version of DNS it is easy to recognize the feasibility of implementing governance. Only relatively minor medications would be needed to realize the four mechanisms of authority, law, sanctions, and jurisdictions. The DNS defines a central authority for the Internet.

The uniqueness requirement of the name space requires a single central authority, and its decisions apply to all servers in the name space. To render the DNS policy authority a true regulatory entity, its domain of decision making would simply have to expand to public issues, such as intellectual property regulation or content control. Since there are few technical barriers to such an expansion, it would be a policy choice. Thus, realizing governance on the Internet would require simply broadening the range of topics regulated by the DNS policy authority.

The DNS also defines the second governance mechanism law. The law of the Internet is contained in the domain name registration contracts. The provisions of the contracts with network administrators specify the detailed regulations for their actions. To regulate on broader topics, the language in the contracts would simply have to expand. Third, DNS provided a powerful mechanism for sanctions: domain name denial (i.e., the deletion of a user's name–number listing from the name space). This is the power of banishment : Network administrators who refused to obey the regulations in their contracts could be delisted from the name space and made to disappear. Name registration could be treated as a privilege, revocable if a user violated the rules.

The DNS neatly solves the problem of jurisdiction as well. The jurisdiction of the DNS policy authority extends to every computer on the Internet but no farther. The registration contract is the manifestation of jurisdiction . Every network administrator is contractually bound to the DNS's policy authority. Thus, the domain name system provided the means to realize mechanisms of governance. Relatively minor changes to DNS could put each mechanism in place. The DNS policy authority would need to merely broaden its regulatory scope and include those broader regulations in contracts with network administrators. Domain name denial provides an adequate mechanism to sanction rule breakers. The jurisdiction of the policy authority would exactly cover the Internet, no less and no more. In order to fully realize Internet governance, two additional considerations would have to be addressed. The practical some means would be needed to extend policy authority to the individual user. Since the domain name registration contract is between the central authority and a network administrator, individual users are not immediately subject to regulations.

Regulation of individual users could be achieved using a *flow-down contrac*t administrators generally require users to sign an agreement when they obtain an account, and this user contract could repeat the provisions from the administrators' contract. In this way a single set of regulations cou'd "'flowdown" from the central DNS administrator to network administrator sand from there to all users. Indirectly, all Internet users could be regulated by the central DNS administrator. Violation of the user contract could lead to loss of Internet access for the user account.

Network administrators who failed to enforce ' flow-down contracts on their users would" and themselves subject to domain name denial, that is, banishment from the Internet. A second consideration about governance is more normative in nature. Were the DNS policy authority to become a general-purpose regulator, then careful thought would have to be given to its *legitimacy*. As the scope of its policymaking expanded, its authority would have to be grounded on some appropriate principle. This could be realized by placing ultimate policy authority in the hands of governments or in the hands of a newly constituted representational institution. As discussed later, when policy authority was located in ICANN, it adopted a representational mechanisms to ensure legitimacy.

The discussion so far has built on one simplifying assumption: that the Internet name space is a single, centralized database. In the early phases of the Internet's development this was true. In the 1970s the entire name space was contained in one called "hosts.txt". By 1983, however, the continued growth of the network had led researchers to redesign the name space, and break up the name space into multiple, interconnected pieces. The name space is less centralized than has been presented here. Decentralization renders governance of the Internet much more complex.

DNS and Governance

In fact, the name space is a *distributed* database. In theory, all name–number pairs could be held in one central database as described in the simplied account just given. However, since thousands of name resolution queries occur each second, a centralized DNS computer might be over whelmed. Instead, the name space is distributed among multiple computers to share the workload. The name space exists as a collection of partial, separate databases running on separate computers. Each partial database is called a *zone* (or *zon*e). A zone contains a subset of the total list of name–number pairs. To each zone is associated a *name server* (or *serve*r—a software program for name resolution) and a *host computer* (or *hos*t—the hardware that hosts the zone and name server). Thus, the entire name space is a distribute d database-and-name-resolution system whose building block is the triad of a zone name server program, and host computer.

As in any distributed database, the relationship between the parts is carefully structured. The different zone are linked to each other to form a top-down pyramidal hierarchy or an inverted tree (with its root at the top). At the apex of the hierarchy is a single zone, the *root*. The root zone links to multiple zones just beneath it, and those zones in turn link to multiple zones beneath them, and soon. (This is the same structure as the file on a personal computer). The levels in the hierarchy are clearly identified: The root zone links to "top-level" zones, these link to "second-level" zones, then the "third-level" zones, and so on. While a given zone may link downward to multiple zones, it can link upward to just one zone. Directly or indirectly, all zones link upwards to the single root zone. The existence of one root in the name space full is the uniqueness condition.

Subtrees in this distributed database are called *domains. A* domain consists of a zone and all zones beneath it in the hierarchy. Domain names are often referred to by their level in the tree. Domains beginning at top-level zones are top-*level domains* or TLDs; domains beginning at the next level are *second-level domains*, and so on. The domain of the root is the complete name space. The entire system constitutes the domain name system or DNS. The terms zone and *domain* are often used interchangeably, but the former refers to one single "file and the latter refers to that single file and all lower "file in its subtree.

A domain has a name—which, not surprisingly, is called a *domain name*. Well-known top-level domain names are.com, .org, and .net. The largest domain in the name space.com links to millions of lower-level domains. An Internet address like mycomputer.com consists of a second-level domain (my computer) and a top-level domain (.com). A string of domain names, with the different levels separated by dots, uniquely identifies any computer in the name space.

This distributed hierarchy defines relationships of top-down control. Any zone file can be modified to link (include) or delink (exclude) the zones below it in the name space. This is the power of virtual life and death. When a name server is connected to the root via some series of links, then it exists in the name space. Should a zone eliminate a link, the computer or computers below it in the hierarchy will be cut off from the name space. Each server in the hierarchy controls the path to the root for the servers below it.

A registry in Virginia maintains a zone file called .com, a registry in England maintains a zone file called .uk, my parent company hosts a zone is called holding company (which is itself linked to the .com zone file). By my registering my host into an available zone file, it becomes part of the name space and exists in the Internet. Likewise, should my entry in the zone file ever be delinked (the domain name cancelled), my host would disappear from the Internet. The modication to the zone file that allows me to enter or exit from the Internet is not made by me but by the administrator of the next higher zone file.

In the simplified explanation earlier, DNS administration and policy authority were held by a single pair of organizations. In the distributed DNS, every domain has such an administration – policy pair. These organizations are organized according to the distributed structure of the name space: Total DNS administration is a multiorganization hierarchy, with each administrator exercising control over lower level administrators. At the apex of the hierarchy is the root administrator.

Each administrator exercises monopoly control over its immediate zone file (to ensure uniqueness of its portion of the name space). Moreover, each administrator has authority over the entire domain beneath it. When it registers a lower level host, it delegates some authority to the lower level administrator, who exercises monopoly control over that lower zone file. Authority flows down the hierarchy from the root zone administrator, with responsibility for the entire name space, to the individual host computers at the lowest level zones. Each administrator is subject to the policies of higher level entities. In this way, the policies made at the root can be transmitted down through the levels of the hierarchy to apply, directly or indirectly, to all administrators in the DNS. As a group, the administrators serve as the gatekeepers to the name space and hence to the Internet.

Just as zone are joined by links, administrators are joined by contracts. The root administrator formalizes its delegation of authority to top-level administrators in a contract. Some provisions of that contract may be required to be included in subsequent contracts. In this way, regulations may dow down the entire hierarchy to the individual network administrator or possibly even the individual user, as discussed earlier.

As one would expect, the administration of the root zone is particularly important. All other hosts on the Internet access the name space only with a delegation of authority directly or indirectly from the root. Policy authority over the root—the power to add or delete top-level domains—confers direct control over all top-level domains and indirect power over all lower level domains. Authority over the root zone extends to the entire Internet.

In summary, this more accurate account of the DNS reveals another order of magnitude of technical and administrative complexity. Seen as a whole, the DNS is a centralized control point for the Internet. However, because it is a decentralized system, the DNS has an internal structure that relies on hierarchical control and contracts to achieve unified policy capabilities.

Factors in DNS

At this point we can switch from technical analysis to historical analysis. The discussion so far outlined the functioning of the DNS and its structure as a distributed data-base. This historical analysis outlines evolution of the DNS name space and its administrative hierarchy.

The Internet began as a research project in the 1970s, and the computer scientists developing it shaped the evolution of its administrative and policy institutions. This research community was centered in institutions like the Internet Engineering Task Force (IETF), the Internet Architecture Board (IAB), the University of Southern California's Information Sciences Institute (ISI), and the Internet Society (ISOC).

One person, in particular, played a key role in the DNS development: Dr. Jon Postel, a computer scientist at the University of Southern California. Working under a research contract from the US government, Postel exercised policy authority over the root, a function eventually called the Internet Assigned Number Authority (IANA). In his IANA role, Postel maintained the root zone " le, authorized the addition of new top-level domains (TLDs), selected administrators to whom to delegate authority, and performed myriad other tasks. Postel had first assumed this task as a graduate student in the 1970s. As the Internet grew, the significance of Postel's decisions increased accordingly, and by the 1990s his decisions had global implications. Yet policy authority over the root continued to reside in him personally. Since he worked as a government contractor, final authority of officially lay with the U.S. government—but for most of the 1980s and 1990s, Postel exercised personal authority over the DNS.

In 1984, in a document known as RFC920, Postel and colleague Joyce Reynolds defined the evolutionary trajectory of the name space defined the number of top-level zones and the names they would bear. While the name space would always have just one root zone file, Postel and Reynolds announced in 1984 that the top level would consist of some 250 zone files. RFC920 served as the blueprint for the structure of the name space and its future growth. This number of zone files had no basis in technical necessity; it could have been smaller or larger.

RFC920 also specified the character strings to identify the zone files. The 250 TLDs would be divided into two naming classes: There would be six "generic" TLDs TLDs: .gov, .edu, .com, .org, .mil, and .net), and there would be some 244 "country code" TLDs. Again, the particular character strings used in the domain names had no technical significance; they merely had to be unique. However, as chosen, the strings had major policy significance, for their meaning simplied that different zones would have different uses. The 250 TLDs defined a name space partly based on function (.com for commercial, .mil for military, etc.) and partly based on geopolitical identifiers (country names). Decided long before the Internet's global significance emerged, the number of TLDs and the meanings attached to them would have lasting consequences.

While RFC920 defined the DNS structure and naming conventions, its implementation proceeded incrementally over many years. Implementation of the TLDs required selecting an administrator to maintain the zone file and to operate the name server. Furthermore, the implementation of the generic TLDs proceeded very differently than the country code TLDs: The U.S. government selected the former, while IANA selected the latter.

While Postel/IANA possessed policy authority over the root, the administrator of the root was a private company: Network Solutions, Inc. (NSI). NSI took its orders from IANA, but ultimately operated under contract with the US government. NSI both administered and exercised policy authority over .com, .net, and .org.

Growth in .com made NSI both wealthy and powerful. After the U.S. government opened the Internet to commercial use in 1994, registrations in .comexploded. By the late 1990s, .com had grown to over 10 million registrations—more than half of the entire name space. This concentration of growth in the name space was not an inherent feature of the DNS, but rather occurred as an unfore seen development—a combination of good marketing by NSI and widespread acceptance of the DNS naming convention, which identified .com as the commercial domain.

Ultimately, the .com domain contained so much of the total name space that it rivaled the root for its importance for the overall network. Charging an annual fee of $35 per registered name, NSI collected hundreds of millions of dollars of revenue from its monopoly of the Internet's one commercially named domain. In contrast to NSI, administrators of country code TLDs resembled IANA: They were usually nonprotect organizations, often affiliated with university research centers. Since IANA had defined zone files in terms of country codes and had created just one zone file per country, there was just one administrator in each country. Each of them constituted an implicit national monopoly: the .fr registrywas France's only registry, the .uk registry was the sole UK registry, and so on.

Although there was no technical basis for national monopolies, the naming convention in RFC920 implied such a system. Organizationally, the system of national ccTLD monopolies was reminiscent of the system of national telephone companies (PTTs), which operated as national monopolies in many countries. By October 2000 the full name space consisted of over 30 million name–number pairs. Since IANA had not expanded the number of top-level domains since issuing RFC920, most growth in the name space occurred in second-level domains. Most of that was contained in a single TLD, .com, where NSI had registered over 18 million hosts. NSI's .org and .net TLDs contained another 5 million hosts. The rest of the name space was mostly distribute d in various country code TLDs. Aboveit all, Jon Postel at IANA oversaw delegations of authority to new administrators .

Thus the DNS as it existed toward the end of the 1990s was considerably more complex than the system described earlier. First, it was decentralized. The change from hosts.txt to the decentralized DNS occurred in 1983.

Second, over the years numerous non technical developments had shaped the system. Most TLDs bore country code identifiers, which associated them with geopolitical entities (countries). One zone file in the hierarchy, .com, contained nearly the entire name space (thereby somewhat defeating decentralization). In the community of nonprotect DNS administrators , Network Solutions was emerging as a commercial giant. Most importantly, policy authority for the entire DNS lay with one person, Jon Postel. The DNS was complex—and rife with potential conflicts.

Nonetheless, the DNS could still be used to realize the mechanisms of governance. Although more complex arrangements would be needed than those discussed earlier, a decentralized DNS could still be used to realize authority, law, sanctions, and jurisdictions.

Decentralization would not significantly affect the realization of two mechanisms: law and sanctions. Even with the addition of multiple levels of hierarchy, 'flow-down contracts could still bring rules down to users. Decentralization would require a longer cascade of flow-down contracts but would not otherwise affect this mechanism. Likewise, domain name denial could still serve as a sanction. With each administrator in the name space, from the root on down, exercising monopoly control over its zone file, each one could delink lower level hosts from the name space. Name registration could still be treated as a privilege, revocable if a registrant violated the rules.

Decentralization would render the other two governance mechanisms considerably more difficult to realize, however. Decentralization fragmented authority and jurisdiction, especially in the country code domains.

Policy authority and jurisdiction would still be unified at the root. IANA could make rules for the entire name space and promulgate them down the hierarchy. However, at the top-level domains (TLDs) it would encounter another authority that might challenge it. The distinction between generic TLDs (gTLDs) and country code TLDs (ccTLDs) would inhibit unity of authority and jurisdiction.

ccTLDs are associated with countries, and most countries already have policy authorities: their national governments. National governments could claim jurisdiction in ccTLDs bearing their country code. Although national governments' domains were lower in the DNS hierarchy than IANA, it would be awkward for IANA to assert authority over them. An Internet governance institution would be in a poor position to challenge a national government's right to make public policy. Even if a national government was unaware of the DNS (as was often the case), the proactive exercise of policy authority by IANA might provoke a national government to act. Thus it would be difficult for the policy authority at the root to exercise policy authority in the ccTLDs.

Making matters more complex, among the ccTLDs there would be a plethora of authorities. Country code TLDs were independent from each other, and each could make its own policies in its domain, potentially resulting in a host of divergent and conflicting policies. Decentralization of the DNS had created hundreds of authorities, each with an implicit claim of jurisdiction over their ccTLD. Thus it would seem that integrated governance of the Internet would be impossible. The engineers' decision to organize the name space according to politic allines, as codified in RFC920, had fragmented authority and jurisdiction.

In the gTLDs, in contrast, integrated governance would be possible. IANA could regulate domains like .com, .org,and .net, because these domains had no accountability to authorities outside of the DNS. Any authority they possessed in the DNS was only by way of a delegation from IANA. Furthermore, although gTLDs were only a small number of the total set of domains, they contained the lion's share of all users. Effective authority in just these domains would still affect most Internet users.

Thus fully integrated governance would not be possible in the DNS—but a workable degree of governance would be. The realization of a single authority and a single jurisdiction in .com, .org, and .net would be straightforward. Moreover, such a jurisdiction would include most users, given the heavy concentration of registrations in the gTLDs. Policy authority at the root could regulate them by flow-down contracts backed by the threat of domain name denial. This would reduce but not overcome the problem of fragmented authority.

To further mitigate the fragmentation of authority, IANA and national governments could seek to coordinate policies. Although there were hundreds of ccTLDs, registrations were unevenly distribute d among them. Domains like.uk or .jp contained many more registrations than others like .bg (Bulgaria). Coordination between IANA and just the largest ccTLDs would bring the Internet much closer to integrated governance by bringing most of the outstanding users under the same policies.

One could speculate that additional policy coherence could be achieved by pressuring any recalcitrant ccTLD authorities. Were a small ccTLD to resist enforcing some policy backed by IANA and by large governments, the larger parties could challenge the policy authority of the smaller national governments. IANA could exercise its ability to delink a top-level domain or reassign it to a more compliant administrator. In this way, smaller ccTLDs might be coaxed or bullied into adopting policies agreed on by larger players. Overall policy coherence would be improved.

In closing this section, a final issue must be addressed: the role of the U.S. government. The U.S. government employed Jon Postel and Network Solutions, and it claimed" final authority over the root zone file. Although IANA was the highest policy authority in the DNS, IANA itself operated under policy authority of the United States. Were Internet governance mechanisms to be implemented, and were the status of the United States not to change, then the United States would be the final authority over the Internet. This again might cause tensions with other national governments, which would find themselves subordinate to the United States.

In summary, a decentralized DNS would not allow for full realization of mechanisms of governance. Law and sanctions could be easily realized, but authority and jurisdiction would be fragmented. Located in the gTLDs, most users could be regulated by IANA. Bringing the entire name space under IANA's authority, however, would require negotiation with many autonomous national authorities.

ICANN

Having reviewed the DNS, we can now turn to the Internet Corporation for Assigned Names and Numbers (ICANN). Created in 1998 and still evolving at the time of this writing, ICANN realizes the governance potential in DNS, lever aging Internet addressing to achieve global governance. Not only has it created the capabilities for regulation, it has even employed them: In 1999 ICANN promulgated global public policy that defined intellectual property rights in domain names.

By the late 1990s the DNS had come under severe stress from a variety of sources. The Internet had rapidly outgrown its original institutions , most notably the very personal nature of IANA, whose legitimacy was based on the reputation of one man. Should something have happened to Jon Postel, IANA could have become unstable. Another source of stress arose from entrepreneurs wishing to compete with NSI's monopoly: They began proposing alternate name spaces, new TLDs (e.g., .web), and independent registries. This threatened to fragment the name space.

The global nature of IANA was another issue. The United Nations' International Telecommunications Union (ITU) became involved and sought to assume authority over the name space. National governments and the European Commission became interested, too; they perceived a threat to their sovereignty from U.S. control of this new global information infrastructure. Disputes over sovereignty and jurisdiction were heating up. Intense conflicts also began to emerge over domain names that matched trademarks (e.g., coca-cola.com). The United Nations' World Intellectual Property Organization

(WIPO) and U.S. interest groups applied intense political pressure to install trademark regulations in domain names. Making this political mix all the more volatile was that these conflicts developed in "Internet time"; every passing month witnessed exponential growth in the size of both the network and the political stakes.

The process by which the research community, trade mark interests, communication businesses, and national governments came together to create a new institution tore place IANA is documented elsewhere. Here we are interested in the product of that long and contentious process: ICANN.

ICANN is best understood as a set of semi-autonomous institutions. That set includes not only ICANN as a corporation but also some external entities like a committee of national governments and the TLD administrators. The four mechanisms of governance are mixed deep in ICANN's administrative system and so can be difficult to identify. In what follows, analyse ICANN's features in terms of their governance-related functions.

The new ICANN corporation replaced Jon Postel as the policy authority over the root. ICANN solved the problem of stability: A person was replaced by an institution, so that the IANA could function independently of any one individual. ICANN also partially solved the problem of intergovernmental conflict: ICANN was private, and its by law sex plicitly for bade government officials from serving on the board. Thus although its authority would extend globally, that authority was ostensibly nongovernmental and would not conflict with national governments' sovereignty. Furthermore, with a mission to engage in simple technical coordination of the Internet, ICANN claimed to have no public policy role.

The problem of legitimacy was addressed by the composition of the board of directors. A person, Postel, was replaced by a collection of representatives; legitimacy through expertise and personal reputation was replaced by legitimacy through accountability to stakeholders. ICANN's board represented different functional and geographic constituencies. Of 19 directors, 9 represented technical expert groups, another 9 represented users, and the final director was the organization's top staff person.

ICANN's board, however, was itself subject to a higher authority: the U.S. government. The U.S. Department of Commerce (DOC) retained ultimate control of the root, leaving ICANN policy decisions subject to a potentialve to. Despite the much-publicized privatization, the United States never completely ceded its hold over the Internet. As an official "fact sheet" of the DOC stated, "The Department of Commerce has no plans to transfer to any entity its policy authority to direct the authoritative root server". Thus the Internet was international and privatized but only under the watchful over sight of the U.S. government. (Whether the United States will eventually cede full authority to ICANN is not currently known.)

Beneath the root, contracts extended the authority of ICANN and the United States down to the administrators of the gTLDs and the ccTLDs. The generic TLDs proved more willing to sign on, since NSI administered nearly all of them and was under pressure from the United States to participate in ICANN. Following some bargaining over conditions NSI and ICANN reached agreement in 1999. ICANN thereby achieved policy authority in the most populous domains. The ccTLDs proved more circum spect, and as late as 2001 ICANN was still reporting small progress in this area. Top-down policy authority in these domains failed to be established and remained one of the most difficult issues in the system.

The implicit conflict of authority between ICANN and national governments manifested itself in the Governmental Advisory Committee (GAC). The GAC was an official ICANN advisory committee in which national governments could meet, discuss, and coordinate their actions. Individually, each national government could assert policy authority over the zone file bearing its country code .Together, in GAC, the national governments could coordinate policy.

GAC's first acts were to establish the legitimacy of members' claims to policy authority. First, GAC declared," The Internet naming system is a public resource in the sense that its functions must be administered in the public or common interest". By defining the DNS as a public good, similar to electromagnetic spectrum, GAC prepared they way for governmental oversight. Then GAC linked that public interest to national governments' authority: "ultimate public policy authority over the relevant country code domain] rests with the relevant government". This justified the claim by national authorities that ccTLD domains were under their jurisdiction.

Thus ccTLD administrators found themselves under two authorities—and they asserted a third of their own. ICANN claimed that ccTLDs' authority derived from its higher authority over the root; if administrators did not flow-low ICANN's policies, ICANN could redelegate authority to another party. For their part, national governments claimed that their zone file was a public resource under their authority. A third approach was backed by ccTLD administrators, who cited policy documents that located authority in the "local Internet community" rather than in ICANN or in governments. This prescription would render the administrator s accountable to Internet users in their home country rather than to their government or ICANN.

GAC members sought to resolve this ambiguity in their favour by requesting from ICANN a veto power over ccTLDs similar to the U.S. power over the root. GAC proposed that ICANN's power of redelegation be given to national governments: "when ICANN is notified by the relevant government or public authority that the [administrator] has contravened the terms . . . ICANN should act with the utmost promptness to reassign the delegation". Country code managers would have access to the root only as long as their national government allowed it. ICANN resisted this arrangement, which would have subordinated it to national governments. At the time of this writing the fragmentation of authority over the ccTLDs remained unresolved.

The GAC forum allowed national governments to coordinateon a variety of other policies. GAC began developing a "best practice" document for country managers, so that national authorities could standardize their operations. Once common policies were defined, each national government could promulgate and enforce those practices in its own jurisdiction.

Thus the multiplicity of authorities caused jurisdictional fragmentation. ICANN claimed jurisdiction over the entire name space and, hence, over all users. Likewise, the U.S. jurisdiction extended over ICANN and so over the entire name space. At the top level of the name space, however, jurisdictional conflicts merged. The jurisdictions defined by the generic TLDs posed little problem; there ICANN prevailed. In the country code TLDs, however, national governments claimed jurisdiction. This prevented ICANN and the United States from realizing one unified jurisdiction in the name space. Still, the vast majority of Internet users found themselves in ICANN's sole jurisdiction.

Although ICANN regulated users, it did not have direct contact with users. Instead, a four tiered system was implemented, with ICANN at the top, users at the bottom, and two kinds of organization—registries and *registrars* —in between. At the top ICANN used its authority to make regulations. Beneath it, registries maintained the zone files and operated the servers (as described earlier). Beneath the registries came the registrars, who served as the retail interface to users. They performed customer-oriented tasks of leasing and servicing domain names to users, often bundling these with additional services like Internet service provision. Finally, at the bottom tier were users (or network administrators, who, in turn, contracted with individual users).

Flow down contracts spanned these levels. ICANN's regulations were embodied in contracts with registries, which included the regulations in their contracts with registrars, who included them in their contracts with network administrators. Policies "flowed down" from ICANN to registries to registrars and ultimately to private networks. The terms of the contract defined the laws of the Internet.

At each level, ICANN backed up contracts with the threat of domain name denial. Registries who disobeyed could have their domain redelegated. Registrars who disobeyed could lose their access to registries, so they would no longer be able to offer domain names to users. Users who disobeyed could have their domain names removed from the name space or assigned to someone else.

ICANN's Registrar Accreditation Contract was the primary mechanism for promulgating law. Any organization that wished to serve as a registrar had too bey the terms of this contract. It included an open-ended requirement: "Registrar shall comply . . . with all ICANN- adopted Policies" As ICANN policies changed and the accreditation agreement evolved so could the conditions imposed on domain name usage. It was this contractual blank check that most clearly gave ICANN the right to exercise broad governance activities. The contract's provisions had to be repeated in lower level contracts between registrars and users, guaranteeing that regulations would flow from ICANN to the registrars and eventually to users. These regulations were enforceable with clear sanctions: "The [domain name] holder shall agree that its registration of the [domain] name shall be subject to suspension, cancellation, or transfer pursuant to any ICANN- adopted policy . . . for the resolution of disputes".

Thus the basic governance mechanisms were flow down contracts backed up by domain name denial. The accreditation contract stipulated the regulations for the Internet, and the power to revoke domain names provided the sanction for enforcement. Internet users could only enjoy access to the name space if they obeyed

ICANN's rules; if they broke the rules, they could see their domain name suspended, cancelled, or transferred.

Global Public Policy

The preceding discussion of DNS, governance, and ICANN's institutional design has been largely descriptive and analytical. What is reviewed here is mostly established fact. If one accepts the four part definition of governance, and if one admits that those mechanisms are indeed present in ICANN, then it is not controversial to state that ICANN has the capability to engage in Internet governance. So far, little has been said about whether ICANN exercises that capability or whether the system of governance is legitimate.

ICANN not only has the capacity to govern, it has also done so. ICANN has made global public policy. Shortly after ICANN's governance capabilities were implemented, they were put into practice. In August 1999 ICANN promulgated its first major policy: the Uniform Dispute Resolution Policy (UDRP), which mandated a procedure for deciding who has intellectual property rights in a domain name (ICANN, 1999 b). The UDRP illustrates how ICANN's governance mechanisms work in practice. The UDRP also constitute s ICANN's first global public policy.

In the late 1990s domain names became valuable, with names like yahoo.com and amazon.com becoming important business assets. As the value of domain names rose, disputes arose over name rights. Some disputes arose when individual s allegedly registered trademarks in anticipation of selling them to their owner; other arose when owners allegedly attempted to wrest control over desirable characterstrings from other users. Sometimes ownership rights conflicted with rights of fair use or free speech. The trouble with such conflicts was that existing trademark law was inadequate for many disputes: Trade mark law was national, whereas many disputes were international. Legal mechanisms to settle international disputes in domain names were expensive and awkward to employ.

ICANN's UDRP defined procedures for resolving domain name disputes, thereby effectively setting rules of ownership and property. Disputes would be settled through an alternative dispute resolution procedure, in which certified private arbitrators would decide the question of rights based on criteria defined by ICANN. Arbitration decisions could be enforced by removal or transfer of the disputed name. It was a "voluntary" system in that parties who were unsatisfied by the outcome of arbitration could still resort to existing judicial forums for judgment. However, since existing forums were extremely costly, the UDRP would in most cases provide the final decision on property rights. The UDRP had de facto the force of law.

The implementation of the Uniform Dispute Resolution Policy (UDRP) illustrates ICANN's use of all four governance mechanisms. First, the UDRP was developed with input from staff and various parties and ultimately approved by the ICANN Board in an exercise of its authority. Second, the policy was codified into law through the Registrar Accreditation Agreement. ICANN made the UDRPa condition for registrar access to the name space, and registrars had to include the UDRP in their retail contracts with users (it had to flow down"). Third, the UDRP included sanctions: Users who refused to agree to the policy in advance were denied access to the name space, and users who were found to be in violation of the UDRP could have their names deleted or reassigned (banishment). Finally, the UDRP applied in ICANN's jurisdiction. The policy regulated domain name usage in the .com, .net, and .orgdomains. In country code domains, where ICANN's authority did not immediately apply, the decision to adopt the UDRP lay with country code administrators . At the time of this writing, the policy had been adopted in some domains but not in all.

In making the UDRP, ICANN made global public policy. The UDRP regulates something of public value: rules of property. Rules of property, such as trademark, copyright, and intellectual property, are traditionally made by governments. The U.S. Constitution , for instance, specifies rules of intellectual property protection in patents. At the global level, the reason for a lack of regulation is not that property rules are somehow less public, but that there has been no recognized public institution to make such rules. ICANN stepped into this void. By making global rules on property, ICANN made a decisions on public values. Although the UDRP may not have been a policy of enormous import—property rights in domain names is a relatively small area of regulation—it was a significant first step into policymaking.

If ICANN makes global public policy, then it is appropriately evaluated by such policy criteria as legitimacy, accountability, and equity. Indeed, it is around issues like these that most controversies have erupted. Here, briefly review some of the issues that have arisen around the ICANN board's legitimacy.

U.S. policy for the creation of ICANN was laid out in the Department of Commerce "White Paper," which defined principles for ICANN. Two principles there were particularly relevant to legitimacy: ICANN should be committed to "private, bottom-up coordination," and it should be committed to "representation . . . [providing] input from the broad and growing community of Internet users". Some of these principles became embodied in ICANN's by laws, especially in the mechanisms for representation on the board.

In a number of instances these principles of legitimacy were not convincingly upheld. In a move that generated considerable public out cry (and hearings in the U.S. Congress), the first set of interim directors was appointed with no public participation or consultation. Instead, the selection process was conducted behind closed doors in a process later described even by Jon Postel as "undemocratic and closed". However, it was this board that promulgated the Uniform Dispute Resolution Policy.

The ICANN board was also implemented unevenly. The directors for the nine expert representatives were seated within approximately 1 year of ICANN's creation, and those directors quickly moved to weaken the seats reserved for Internet user representatives. In a series of board meetings in 1999 and 2000, the appointed and expert directors sought to eliminate, reduce, or delay the implementation of the elected directors (Klein, 2000a). In so doing, they repeatedly revised the corporate bylaws that constrained board actions. As one top government official declared to them at their meeting in July 2000, "the Board is increasingly giving the impression of being extremely cavalier in changes to the bylaws". Shortly thereafter, the board decided to modify the bylaws again to defer the final round of director elections until 2002—fully 4 years after the creation of ICANN.

Finally, ICANN's early board gave evidence of preferring industry professionals to represent Internet users. In the first, partial round of director elections, the board" labelled most of the nominee slots for user representatives with candidates of its own choosing, selecting individuals from telecommunications giants like France Telecom, Fujitsu, Deutsche Telekom, and Verizon. This tendency to favour the telecommunications supply industry over Internet users attracted the notice at ICANN's July 2000 meeting, of an Australian government official, who stated, "[ICANN] runs the risk of potentially becoming a de facto industry association". The legitimacy of the board to make decisions affecting all Internet users was again weakened by this tendency for some interest groups to seek (and arguably to achieve) disproportionate influence on the board.

With ICANN making global public policy, its lack of legitimacy was striking. Although the elections of 2000 brought some user representation to ICANN, they fell short of implementing the degree of representation called for in ICANN's original bylaws.

Institutions are not static entities; they grow over time and often expand their areas of activity. Such seems likely for ICANN. As an Internet governance entity, what policies might ICANN promulgate in the future?

Perhaps the most likely area of policy expansion is in intellectual property protection. Such expansion of rights has been actively championed since the beginning of the ICANN process and would be consistent with the initial direction of ICANN's activities. The UDRP could be expanded to give special registration rights to owners of celebrity names, famous marks, geographical names, and so on. ICANN could become a global regulator in the service of property and e-commerce.

Control over the name space could also be leveraged to promote social justice. ICANN and ccTLD monopolies could raise funds for a universal service fund to overcome the global digital divide, allowing poorer countries to pay less for Internet access than wealthy countries. In private conversations with this author, some ICANN directors from developing countries have supported such policies.

ICANN's capabilities could also be used for content regulation. Sites violating content regulations could be censored by having their domain names revoked or redirected. Domain name denial was used in this way in the case of voteauction.com, which operated a site containing illegal content (an online mechanism for the buying and selling of votes). The registrar for the domain cancelled the registration to suppress its content. In theory, ICANN could enforce regulations broadly using similar mechanisms.

ICANN could become a vehicle for taxation, perhaps serving as a means whereby governments collected commerce taxes or whereby ICANN funds its own initiatives. With domain names available from one sole source, users would have to either pay the fee or suffer denial of access. Indeed, both U.S. legislators and disgruntle d ccTLDs have accused ICANN of levying taxes.

Finally, ICANN could become a vehicle for U.S. national policy. In times of war or terrorism, countries opposing the United States could see their domains removed from the Internet. Individual registrations could be cancelled or redirected to reduce the effectiveness of hostile entities. The relationship between ICANN policy and U.S.national policy had already come up when the U.S. Department of Commerce had approved the addition of the.ps domain—for Palestine—to the root zone. Although the United States did not pursue its narrow national interest, the case attracted attention because of the potential for conflict.

With governance mechanisms in place, the possibility of mission creep—the steady expansion of ICANN's regulatory scope—seems possible. The combination of effective mechanisms for governance and weak mechanisms for legitimacy could allow some parties to make global public policies that favour their interests.

The simple recognition that ICANN engages in Internet governance is significant. It contradicts established beliefs and it raises concerns about what kind of governance is being established. It forces us to ask what should be done. ICANN contradicts the popular myth of a be nevolent Internet anarchy. As it turns out, the Internet *can* be controlled. The DNS provides a basis for top-down control, and ICANN leverages that to make policy. The implications of this are far-reaching and will only be seen overtime. For this reason, ICANN's future should concern all Internet users.

In ICANN we see three ways in which technology shapes society.

First, objective features of the technology shaped the administrative and regulatory system. In particular, the technical characteristics of a distributed database set important policy parameters. The need for a single name space with a unique root created a central control point. Likewise, the need for unique identifiers (so that a name identifies just one host computer) created problems of control and monopoly. With just one .com zone, within which there could be registered just one .coca-cola, a system of monopoly registries was created and the basis for trademark fights was laid.

It may be that these technology design features were not absolutely necessary (although convincing alternatives were not advanced even by ICANN's critics). At minimum, however, history rendered those technical features sufficiently embedded that they became equivalent to "necessary." Any attempt to change ICANN's status as regulator may have to begin by redesigning the underlying technology (particularly the requirement for a unique root under the control of a unique administrator).

A second way that technology shaped society was the role of engineers in making policy. The selection of countrycodes as domain names was a historical decision with profound policy consequences. This decision was made so early in the Internet development process that the only participants were research engineers. These engineers decided that Internet domains should be associated with geopolitical entities. Had they selected different alphanumeric identifiers—one could imagine colors, sequential numbers, the table of elements—then there would have been no basis for the one-per-country distribution of registries nor the subsequent assertion of national authority over registries. The engineers decided to organize the Internet like national PTTs. Engineers could make such decisions because they controlled the process early in its developmental history.

A third way that technology influences society is that it provides legitimacy for secretive decision-making. When policy decisions are categorized as "technical," then it becomes legitimate for them to be made behind closed doors by elite groups. Policy disappears from the public sight. The groups that gained control of ICANN invoked this veil of technological legitimacy to discount their critics. Despite having no technical training, ICANN's lawyers justified their actions by claiming that they were making neutral choices on the basis of technical expertise.

Bibliography

Bailey, C.W., 'Public-Access Computer Systems', *Information Technology and Libraries* 12, March 1993.

Burns, T. and Stalker, G. *The Management of Innovation* (2nd edn.). Tavistock, 1968.

Buss Martin D. J. and Lynn M. Salerno, "Common Sense and Computer Security", *Harvard Business Review*, March-April 1984.

Butler, Gathorne. *Organisation and Management*, Prentice Hall, 1986.

Engelberger Joe, *Robotics in Practice* AMACOM, New York and Kogan Page, London, 1981.

Galliers, R. 'Information systems and technology planning within a competitive strategy framework', in *Information Management. State of the Art Report*, P. Griffiths (ed.), Pergamon, 1986.
Kinnucan Paul, "Computers That Think Like Experts", *High Technology*, January 1984, On expert systems..

Lane, Elizabeth S. and Summerhill, Craig A., *An Internet primer for information professionals: a basic guide to networking technology*, Westport, Meckler, 1993.

Leonard-Barton, Dorothy and Kraus, William 'Implementing new technology', *Harvard Business Review*, Nov./Dec. 1985.

Franken, H., *et al.*, *Information Technology and the Law*, Lelystad (Netherlands): Koninklijke Verrmande, 1991.

Janes, J., 'The Internet Public Library'. In *Proceedings of the 101h*

Annual Computers in Libraries International, February 1996. Oxford: Learned Information Europe Ltd, 1996.

Kershner, Lois M., 'Upgrade with Same Vendor', *Information Technology: It's for Everyone: Proceedings of the LITA Third National Conference* (ed.), Thomas W. Leonhardt. Chicago: American Library Association, 1992.

Miller, Danny, 'Evolution and revolution: a quantum view of structural change in organisations', *Journal of Management Studies*, vol. 19, no. 2, 1982.

Malamud, Carl, *Exploring the Internet: a technical travelogue*, London, Prentice-Hall, 1992.

Mandeville Thomas, "The Spatial Effects of Information Technology", *Futures*, February 1983. A review of the literature on possible urban/regional problems.

Owen Kenneth (ed.), *Videotex in Education: A New Technology Briefing* Council for Educational Technology, London, 1982.

Pettigrew, Andrew, *The Politics of Organisational Decision Making*, Tavistock, 1973.

______________, "Information Control as a Power Resource', *Sociology*, vol. 6, issue 2, 1972.

Price Waterhouse Associates (1981), "Review of Economic Implications of Canadian Transborder Data Flows", as reported by *Transnational Data Report*, vol. 4, no. 6.

Toong Hoo-min D. and Amar Gupta, "Personal Computers", *Scientific American*, December 1982.

Shenker, S. *et al.*, 'Pricing in Computer Networks: Reshaping the Research Agenda', *Telecommunications Policy*, vol. 20, 1996.

Index